In the Path of the Explorers

In the Path of the Explorers

TRACING THE EXPEDITIONS

OF VANCOUVER, COOK,

MACKENZIE, FRASER

AND THOMPSON

SHORT & NEERING

Whitecap Books
Vancouver / Toronto

Text by Rosemary Neering
Cover and interior photos by Steve Short
Edited by Elaine Jones
Cover and interior design by Carolyn Deby

Typography by CompuType, Vancouver, B.C.

Printed and bound in Canada by Friesen Printers, Altona, Manitoba

Canadian Cataloguing in Publication Data

Short, Steve.
    In the path of the explorers

    Includes bibliographical references and index.
    ISBN 1-55110-018-5

    1. British Columbia—Discovery and exploration.   2. Northwest, Pacific—Discovery and exploration.   3. Explorers—British Columbia.   4. Explorers—Northwest, Pacific.
I. Neering, Rosemary, 1945-   II. Title.
FC3821.S56 1992   917.11′041   C92-091020-3
F851.5.S56 1992

The publisher acknowledges the assistance of the Canada Council and the Cultural Services Branch of the government of British Columbia in making this publication possible.

The Paths of the Explorers

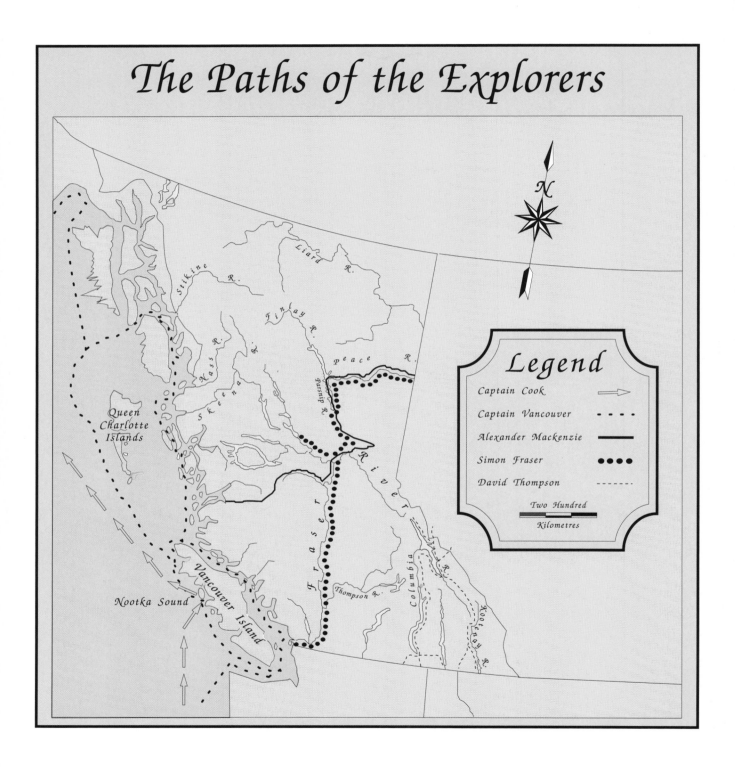

Legend

Captain Cook
Captain Vancouver
Alexander Mackenzie
Simon Fraser
David Thompson

Two Hundred
Kilometres

$\mathcal{C}$ontents

Preface

By the middle of the eighteenth century, the nations of Europe were almost three hundred years into the maritime explorations that had taken their sailors around the world. In those three centuries, they had charted the seas and conquered and exploited the lands that lay in their paths. Every decade, another expedition, another explorer, made their marks on the map of the world.

At stake in this great competition, undertaken mainly by Britain, France, Spain, Russia and Portugal, was the wealth that came from trade with — or the ravaging of — distant regions. Kings and ministers, businessmen, soldiers and sailors vied, under the flag of their country, for the national and commercial superiority that would come from the next great geographic coup.

In the eighteenth century, to the desire to conquer was added the desire to know. The European world was shifting from a theory of knowledge based on speculation to one based on experience and testing. The great Swedish botanist who styled himself Linnaeus had set out the first universal system for the classification of plants, and naturalists competed to be the first to fit exotic plants into that system. Astronomers scanned the skies and made complex mathematical calculations that revealed the size and shape of the universe.

No country was more eager for new conquests and new knowledge than Britain. Ships of the Royal Navy now carried not only sailors and marines, but also

Long Beach, west coast of Vancouver Island. By mid-eighteenth century, the northwest coast of North America was being eyed by European nations eager to explore new regions and expand their trade.

botanists, astronomers and artists. To the usual menagerie stabled aboard ship to feed the crew — or to amuse them — were added sheep, pigs and horses to be established in new colonies. Botanists took aboard seeds that might be grown in new lands, and brought back carefully collected plants for the gardens at Kew.

By the mid-eighteenth century, navigation was still an inexact science: no count exists of the ships lost because of errors in navigation and flawed charts. Violent storms that drove sailors to cut away the masts of their ships, and drift, helplessly, across the seas; winds that thrust vessels ashore or onto rocks; calms that trapped them in bays: the dangers of the sea were endless. And the ships themselves were not healthy places. Hundreds of sailors died of scurvy or of tropical diseases.

In an intensely practical century, sailors and those who sent them across the seas sought better methods of navigation and new ways of keeping ships' crews healthy. The Admiralty announced a prize for the man who could demonstrate a reliable way of determining longitude; soon, inventors came forward with new instruments that they wished the navy to test. Ships' captains were sent forth with a variety of possible cures or preventions for scurvy: portable soup (a kind of bouillon), sauerkraut, essence of malt, the rob or juice of oranges and lemons.

The average British navy ship that sailed the world in the second half of the eighteenth century crowded more than a hundred men below decks, into space that scarcely gave them room to sling a hammock. Many of those men did not want to be at sea at all; they had been impressed into the navy by recruiting gangs that roamed the docks and slums of Britain's ports. "Manned by violence and maintained by cruelty" was a classic description of Britain's navy, where discipline was harsh and lapses swiftly punished. Yet perhaps life afloat was not much worse than life ashore in the slums of the city or fields of the countryside, where casual cruelty could be a way of life, life expectancy was low, and diet was severely restricted. And the chance of seeing new lands and perhaps acquiring valuable goods must have attracted many a sailor.

Though explorers gradually filled in the European map of the world from the sixteenth century on, one blank remained: the North Pacific. Since the days when seamen first sailed across the Atlantic, seeking a route to the fabulous Indies and coming ashore in America, explorers had hunted a passage through the American continents. Charting the Atlantic shores had laid to rest the idea that a passage might exist anywhere between the tip of South America and Newfoundland — but might there yet be a northwest passage? Since the beginning of the sixteenth century, some fifty voyages had been made in search of this supposed Strait of Anian.

Most of these expeditions had begun in the Atlantic. But, in the first half of the eighteenth century, Russian and Spanish explorers had probed north from Mexico and east from Siberia along the Pacific coast of America. In 1728, Vitus Bering sailed through the strait that now bears his name, and lost his life in the service of Russia. In the 1760s and 1770s, Spanish commanders Juan Perez and Juan Francisco de la Bodega y Quadra glimpsed but did not land on parts of Vancouver Island, the Queen Charlotte Islands and Alaska. In 1775, the British Parliament offered twenty thousand pounds to the man who found a northwest passage.

As Europe turned its eyes to the northeast Pacific, explorers by land ventured westward across the continent. Acquiring knowledge may have been one of their motives; profit definitely was their spur. Since the seventeenth century, the Company of Adventurers Trading into Hudson's Bay had welcomed natives bringing furs to their posts along the shores of the bay. Meanwhile, French traders from Montreal had canoed westward, seeking control over the riches of the fur trade. When France lost Canada to Britain in 1763, a new breed of adventurers, many of them Scots, pushed ever farther west.

They travelled in canoes eight metres long, paddled by half a dozen men, in fleets of four or five or more. Each canoe carried more than a tonne of goods, tied up in forty-kilogram packs, two-thirds trade goods, one-third provisions. The voyageurs who manned these canoes were sturdy men, known throughout the northwest as *mangeurs du lard* for their steady diet of salt pork. When they could, they followed the rivers west; when they were blocked by rapids or shallow waters, they heaved their canoes onto their shoulders and portaged, then returned for the packs that they hefted as a lesser man might lift a ten-kilo sack. Relying on natives to guide them along trade routes their guides had long used, and to provide them with game and fish, they established fur-trading territories for the companies that sent them west.

Their arrival and that of the sea-going explorers and traders changed the territory west of the Rockies forever. As long as the newcomers confined themselves to exploration and mapmaking, their relationship with the natives of the region was one of dependence: for food, for path-finding, and for help in a dozen other ways. But the arrival of the early explorers presaged an era of trade and settlement where the relationship between white and native was much less equal, much more exploitative.

In the last decades of the eighteenth century, and the first of the nineteenth, that dark era still lay ahead. In the early years of contact, the explorers learned from the native peoples they travelled and lived with, kept journals, and took observations of the stars, so that they might create accurate maps and charts of the land they crossed and the coast they sailed.

The five who made the greatest contributions to the charting of the land and coast were Captain James Cook and Captain George Vancouver, by sea; and Alexander Mackenzie, Simon Fraser and David Thompson, by land. Though they were far from the first to see this land, or to settle it, their coming and their explorations marked the beginnings of vast change.

In the Path of the Explorers

Captain James Cook: The Last Voyage

Cook encountered many gales on his epic journeys. When a storm threatened, he turned away from land, preferring to take his chances on the open sea than risk being blown onto the rocks.

As night closed in on February 1, 1778, swelling waves drove the *Resolution* away from Niihau, on the Hawaiian Islands. The next morning, in company with the *Discovery*, the *Resolution* sailed north and east, bound for the northwest coast of America.

Accustomed to tropical temperatures, the ships' companies shivered in a climate no cooler than that of England. They were, wrote *Discovery* captain Charles Clerke, "all shaking with Cold here with the Thermometer at 60. I depend upon the assistance of a few good N:Westers to give us a hearty rattling and to bring us to our natural feelings a little, or the Lord knows how we shall make ourselves acquainted with the frozen secrets of the Arctic."

The ships moved across an empty ocean, no point of land, no bird or animal, no scrap of seaweed visible through the waves. The *Resolution*'s carpenters set to work repairing the boats; the sailmakers used

The west coast of Vancouver Island, one of the most notorious stretches of coast in North America, earned the name "Graveyard of the Pacific" for the many ships claimed by its rocks and reefs.

their needles on the sails; the ships' rats gnawed their way through the wooden deck in search of food. "The Sails were got out of the Bread Room," wrote John Gore, the first Lieutenant of the *Resolution* on February 20, "And it Smoak'd with Sulfur: to kill the Cockroaches Families who had been very Troublesome to us. together with their Neighbours the Ratts." Cook wrote little in his diary, just a passing mention of the winds and the ships' position. "If we had not known that the continent of America was not far distant," he mused, "from the few signs we have met with in the vicinity of land, we might have concluded that there was none within some thousand leagues of us, for we have hardly seen a bird or any other oceanic animal since we left the Sandwich Islands."

On February 25, almost a month out of harbour, William Ellis, the ship's surgeon, recorded that they "passed a log of wood with barnacles on it," a sure sign of land somewhere about. "On the 27th, being in the latitude 43 deg. 47 min. N. and longitude 224 deg. 38 min. 30 seconds E," they saw a second log. On March 6, the crew sighted two seals and several whales. As the sky slowly lightened the next morning, the lookout caught his first glimpse of America, and James Cook, recognized by his peers as the greatest living navigator, began his life's last task: to find — or to disprove the existence of — a northern sea passage that linked the Atlantic to the Pacific.

Cook was almost fifty, and at the apex of a long career on the sea when he first saw the coast of northwest America. Practical, determined and inventive, James Cook had spent many years at sea, first aboard

the sturdy Whitby colliers that carried coal through the North and Baltic seas, then with the navy, exploring and charting the St. Lawrence River and the coasts of Newfoundland with such skill and accuracy that the admiral of the fleet praised his "genius and capacity," and ordered him paid an additional fifty pounds for his "indefatigable industry."

When British astronomers announced that Venus would pass between the earth and the sun in June of 1769, the Royal Society and the Admiralty were quick to decide that a British expedition must travel to the South Seas, to calculate by observing the transit the distance of the earth from the sun and the size of the solar system. A second and perhaps more compelling reason underlay the first: Cook and his ships would also explore these seas to prove or disprove the existence of a rumoured southern continent, where Britain might command untold riches. Cook could also test a chronometer just developed, to see whether this instrument designed for determining longitude could withstand the rigours of a long sea voyage. And he would try a variety of antiscorbutics, with the hope that one would prevent scurvy.

On his first voyage, from 1768 to 1771, and in a second that lasted from 1772 to 1774, Cook and his crews swept the southern oceans, exploring and charting the coasts of Australia and New Zealand. On his second voyage, he made three long sweeps into Antarctic waters, probing farther south than anyone had ever done before. "Our ropes were like wires," he wrote in his journal. "Sails like boards or plates of metal and sheaves frozen fast in their blocks so that it required our utmost efforts to get a topsail up or down. The cold is so intense as hardly to be endured." Finally, on January 30, 1774, his way south barred by a solid field of ice, Cook turned back. "I had made the circuit of the Southern Ocean in a high Latitude," he wrote, "and traversed it in such a manner as to leave not the lest room for the Possibility of there being a continent, unless near the Pole and out of the reach of Navigation."

In 1775, the Admiralty determined to mount a new expedition to fill in the map of the northeast Pacific, where uncertain lines based on vague suppositions still took the place of carefully charted coast. Cook, acknowledged as the greatest explorer and one of the finest seamen of his time, was surely the man to head the expedition.

But Cook was now forty-seven, pensioned off and worn down in mind and body. As the winter of 1776 approached, three lords of the Admiralty dined with Cook. No record was kept of their conversation, but by the end of the evening, enthusiasm rekindled, eager once more to see unknown coasts, perhaps spurred by the promise of the twenty-thousand-pound prize, Cook had agreed to lead the expedition. Once more, he would captain HMS *Resolution*, his ship from his second voyage; with the *Resolution* would go a British navy brig, the *Discovery*.

On July 12, 1776, Cook and his men sailed from England, with a motley cargo of provisions and animals: sheep, goats, rabbits, pigs and poultry, as was normal — but also a peacock, a peahen, a bull, two cows, and sundry other livestock, to be presented to the people of Tahiti as gifts from the king.

Their route took them to Capetown, where more beasts, including four horses, were added to the menagerie. "Nothing is wanted," Cook wrote, more whimsically than was his wont, "but a few females of our own species to make the *Resolution* a complete ark" — a deficit usually remedied each time the ship put into port. They continued on to Tasmania and New Zealand. Arriving in the South Pacific too late in the season to tackle the north Pacific coast that year, they lazed away the spring, summer and autumn on the Friendly Islands, Tahiti, Moorea and Raiatea. Finally, in mid-December, 1777, they set sail for the north. Two and a half months later, the *Resolution* and the *Discovery* reached the coast of North America.

Cook calculated their position at latitude 44°33′N, longitude 235°20′E, and recorded land of a moderate height, "hill and vally and almost everywhere covered with wood." The unindented coastline of present-day Oregon offered them no harbour, so they stood off southwest through squalls and rain, waiting for better weather. A day or two of fair weather allowed them closer in, but then squalls, hail and sleet besieged them. The howling northwest winds threatened to drive them on to the shore, where, wrote one crewman, had they not come about, "its highly probable all perished." Clerke showed his frustration: "It is really rather a lamentable business that these Nwters & this very unsettled Wear [weather] shou'd so far intrude upon us, that we can neither forward our Matters by tracing the Coast, nor have the Satisfaction of getting into a Harbour to

"These rains and the close sultry weather they accompany but too often bring on sickness in this passage, one has at least every thing to fear from them, and cannot be too much on ones guard, by obliging the people to dry their cloathes and airing the Ship with fires and smoke at every opportunity."
— August 16, 1776

"We had got pretty near the inlet before we were sure there was one; but as we were in a bay I had resolved to anchor to endeavour to get some Water, of which we were in great want. At length the inlet was no longer doubtfull, at 5 o'clock we reached the west point, where we were becalmed for some time, during which time hoisted out all the boats to tow the Ship in." — March 29, 1778

The snow-capped summits of the Vancouver Island ranges rise above the coast near Nootka Sound. Cook stayed here less than a month — just long enough to repair his ships.

take a look at the Country." Driven offshore, for more than a week they tacked south out of sight of the coast, turning north again only on March 21, when the winds began to blow more gently from the southwest. The following day, they once more caught sight of land.

Cook had been instructed to reach the American coast at about 45 degrees north and proceed to about 65 degrees, "taking care not to lose any time in exploring rivers or inlets or on any other account, until you get to the aforementioned latitude of 65 north." The Admiralty was convinced that any passage must surely lie north of 65 degrees, since exploration of the Atlantic coast showed no passage existed farther south.

But Cook's supplies of wood and water were low, and his vessels in need of repair. He sailed north along the coast, seeking a harbour. "There appeared to be a small opining in the land which flatered us with hopes of finding a harbour,'' Cook wrote — then named the adjoining shore Cape Flattery, for its false invitation. Ironically, fog and wind kept Cook from seeing the true extent of this opening, and here he made one of his few mistakes in geography. The hopes of those who believed in a northwest passage were pinned on the supposed discoveries of two men: Juan de Fuca, a possibly mythical Greek sailor who reported he had discovered a wide opening to the east in the regions where Cook now sailed, and Admiral Bartholomew de Fonte, an explorer cut from the whole cloth woven by a literary prankster. A letter purporting to be from this Admiral of New Spain and Prince of Chili claimed de Fonte had sailed in 1640, at 53 degrees north latitude, far up a river to a lake, another river, another lake and a strait that led him to the Atlantic Ocean. Cook gave no credence to the claims of either man: now in the vicinity of de Fuca's reported discoveries, he declared, "It is this very latitude where we were geographers have placed the pretended Strait of Juan de Fuca, but we never saw nothing like it, nor is there the least probability that iver such thing exhisted." It would take another series of explorers to prove Cook wrong about de Fuca but right about de Fonte.

Dark fell soon after Cook noted the cape. He intended to have another look in the morning, but the Pacific erupted in a hard gale; instead of running in for the land, Cook had to run for his life, driven far out of sight of land. Some evenings, strong west and northwest winds gave way to south winds; though they were always the prelude to storms that blew hardest at

Tide pools all along the coast harbour a wide variety of marine life, some of which provided a welcome source of fresh food for Cook and his crew.

Two hundred years ago, giant Douglas firs were common in the old-growth forests along the coast. Cook commented, as so many others have since, on the proportions of these trees, the biggest he had ever seen.

south-south-east, bringing rain and sleet, Cook was thankful for them, for only these winds permitted the ships to move to the north at all.

A harbour had to be found: the men were now on short rations of two litres of water per person per day. At 9 A.M. on March 29, they espied land again, a long stretch of shore bounded by Estevan Point on the south — named Point Breakers by Cook — and by the blunt, spade-shaped Brooks Peninsula on the north. Perceiving two inlets, Cook went with the wind into the one he named King George's Sound, then later renamed Nootka, believing this to be the Indian name.

The country they now approached was choked with high, snow-capped mountains that were separated by forested valleys and fronted by the sea crashing over sunken rocks. Blessed for once with favourable winds, Cook ordered the *Resolution* towards shore. The winds failed just as they rounded the point, and Cook ordered the sailors into the boats, so that, rowing hard, they could tow the *Resolution* to a safe harbour. The ship anchored in eighty-five fathoms of water, close enough that the men could reach shore with a hawser. The wind failed the *Discovery*; she was forced to anchor just outside the arm until she could draw near the *Resolution* the next day.

Though the Spaniards aboard the ship of Juan Perez were the first Europeans to record seeing the coast of Vancouver Island, the *Resolution* was the first sailing ship to anchor in these waters, its crew the first Europeans to go ashore in the territory of the Nootka people.

The ship was soon surrounded by mas-

sive Nootkan canoes, eleven metres long, close to two metres wide. More than thirty canoes came out to investigate the newcomers: each circled the ship as one man, masked and carrying a spear, stood in the bow and spoke and sang to those aboard the sailing ships. The Nootka made no attempt to come aboard. Instead, they chanted and sang from their canoes. Impressed, the ship's crew brought out two French horns and played two tunes. The Nootka sang again. The ship's company brought out the drum and fife, and closed out the evening's performance with yet more tunes.

In the morning, Cook sent three armed boats to look for a better harbour, then descended himself into a fourth boat to be rowed along the shore of the sound. Seeking a well-protected harbour as far as

"*The land boardering upon the Sea coast is of a middling height and level, but about the Sounds, it consists of high hills and deep vallies, for the most part cloathed with large timber, such as Spruce fir and white Cedar.*" — *April 26, 1778*

Forests once covered the hills around Nootka Sound in a solid cloak of green. Cook found the virgin forest to be a good source of wood for much-needed repairs to his ships.

*In places where some
sun filters through the
thick forest canopy,
dwarf dogwood flowers
and delicate ferns grace
the forest floor.*

possible from the native village, so that neither party should be distracted by the other, he soon found "a pretty snug cove." But it was too late that day to move the ships, so the sailors unbent the sails, struck the masts and spent the rest of the day and evening trading with the Nootka. "A great many Canoes [some counted 94] filled with the Natives were about the ships all day," wrote Cook, "and a trade commenced betwixt us and them, which was carried on with the Strictest honisty on boath sides."

On the next day, the ships were moved to the cove that Cook named Ship Cove; now known as Resolution Cove, it is at the south end of Nootka Sound, on Bligh Island (named for Cook's one-day-to-be-infamous ship's master, William Bligh). Cook planned a short stay, just long enough to find wood to repair the ship and food and water to replenish supplies. He sent ashore wooding and watering parties, and under a tent set up a brewery for "making small Beer with the tops of fir trees" — a specific against scurvy. He placed his observatories on an elevated rock close to the *Resolution*, and sent ashore instruments for scientific observations. The ships' carpenters and blacksmiths set to work making repairs and forging ironwork.

Their refuge, so quickly chosen, was not as well protected as they might have liked. The fine weather of the first week posed no difficulties, but at the beginning of the second week, gales swept down the hills of the island and hammered the ships. "According to the old Proverb," Cook wrote in his journals, "one misfortune seldom comes alone"; under the brunt of the storms, the mizzenmast gave way, and slashing rain forced the carpenters to work under a tent erected over the foremast.

Now the carelessness of the home-port shipwrights who had prepared the *Resolution* and the *Discovery* for their voyage became ever more evident. The cheeks — timbers that support the fore topmast — were rotten, had been defective from the time the ship sailed from England. The cheeks repaired, Cook discovered that the mast itself was so badly damaged that it had to be lifted out and brought ashore for repairs. The projected week's stay became two weeks, then three. The sailors had to replace the decayed lower standard rigging and make a new set of forerigging out of the best of the old main rigging. Then a southeast gale toppled the mizzenmast, revealing it as hideously rotten. A ship's party went in the woods to chop down a tree of suitable girth and height for a new mast. Through hard gales and horizontal rain, the men finished and erected the foremast and finished the rigging on April 16, only to discover that the tree cut down for the mizzenmast was cracked and warped. All hands were ordered back to shore to find and cut a second tree.

Though the delay was intensely frustrating to Cook, it did offer him a chance to become better acquainted with the Nootka. He and those officers of the two ships who kept journals or drew pictures recorded in detail their impressions of the Nootka and their way of life, judging both by the life and customs of Europe. No corresponding Nootkan impressions of the sailors survive, but the journals make it clear that the Nootka were neither cowed nor outmaneuvred by their visitors, whom they treated as equals and regarded as a convenient

The western red cedar was a major component of coastal forests, as were Douglas fir and Sitka spruce.

managing their trade so that "the price of their articles was always kept up while the value of [Cook's] was lessening daily." A week in harbour, the sailors were alarmed when their trading partners suddenly moved to shore and armed themselves with stones and other weapons. But the Nootka soon reassured Cook and his men by signs indicating that they prepared for battle, not with the sailors, but with another group of natives who were approaching by canoe.

Discussions proceeded between the two groups. It was obvious that the local Nootka had taken control of trade with the ships' companies, for no one from outside the original Nootkan group was permitted to trade directly with the ships' crews. At times, the Nootka would disappear for a day or two, returning with new supplies of furs they had presumably acquired from other groups of natives. They also brought supplies of herring, sea perch and cod, most welcome to the ships' companies, who could not, try as they might, catch any fish with hook and line or net.

Each time they returned, they repeated the ceremony of paddling around the ships, greeting and chanting. James Burney, first lieutenant aboard the *Discovery*, was deeply moved by their singing: they gave "3 halloos," he wrote; "the halloo is a single note in which they will all join, swelling it out in the middle and letting the sound die away, in a calm with the hills around us, it had an effect infinitely superior to what might be imagined from anything so simple." The singing was all the more impressive because the Nootka were often silent, unlike the Hawaiian natives, who had battered the sailors with constant, frenetic noise.

source of useful trade goods. Nor do the journals foreshadow the future: though Cook and his men clearly thought the Nootka belonged to an inferior race, for both parties the relationship was fortuitous and transient.

The Nootka offered furs, weapons, bladders of oil, indeed, anything the sailors might accept, in trade for knives, chisels, pieces of iron and tin, nails, metal buttons, bureau ornaments, kettles, pots, candlesticks or any other metal object. Brass was the most sought-after, wrote Cook: "Before we left the place, hardly a bit of brass was left in the Ship, except what was in the necessary implements." The Nootka were little interested in beads, and not at all in any kind of cloth.

The sailors wanted furs; noted one crew member, "nothing is so well-received by us as skins, particularly that of the sea beaver or Otter, the fur of which is very soft and delicate."

Cook found the Nootka astute traders,

*" ʙehind the
ʙruined Village
is a plane of a few
acres covered with some
of the largest trees I ever
saw."* — April 20, 1778

Cook and his men were also becoming more accustomed to the weather, which was, Cook noted on April 26, "infinately milder than on the east coast of America under the same parallel of latitude." Prescient, Cook wrote of the value of the timber in the country: "the wood in general is Fir, there are different kinds of it,

and such a variety in Size, that on going a very inconsiderable distance, you may cut Sticks of every gradation, from a Main Mast for your ship, to one for your Jolly Boat; and these I suppose as good as are to be procur'd in any part of the World." He and those officers who kept diaries commented at length on the absence of game animals

Sitka spruce grow to immense size in the rain-soaked valleys of the west coast. Cook was impressed with the size of the coastal trees, and also used spruce to make spruce beer for his men, a preventive for scurvy.

"We were hardly out of the Sound before the Wind in an instant shifted from NE to SEBE and increased to a Strong gale with Squals and rain and so dark that we could not see the length of the Ship." — April 26, 1778

and birds. They described in detail the Nootka, the countryside, and the weather. "The high mountains which rise on the back & far inland are many of them bare," noted second lieutenant James King, "& serve to heighten & finish the Picture of as wild & savage a Country as one can well draw in so temperate a climate." The ship's artists, John Webber, and the ship's surgeon, William Anderson, drew careful and competent pictures of their surroundings, to be published with the official journals of the voyage.

On April 20, Cook commanded his midshipmen to row him around the sound, stopping at Yuquot where he reported eighty to ninety canoes were drawn up on the beach, and a number of large dwellings housed five to six hundred people. He named the village Friendly Cove, since everyone welcomed him and his men, inviting them into their apartments in the large communal houses. He watched the Nootka women making cedar-bark dresses and cleaning and smoking herring, which they made up into bales and covered with mats. Further up the sound, he saw "some of the largest pine trees you ever saw" — not the last to be confused by the Douglas

A spectacular cloud presages an oncoming storm south of Nootka Sound on Vancouver Island. Cook faced storms such as this with only the most primitive of instruments, but he was armed with years of experience on the high seas.

fir, which is neither pine nor fir. Though the rowing blistered the midshipmen's hands, they were delighted by the break in the weather and in routine. "Captain Cook also on these occasions would sometimes relax from his almost constant severity of disposition, & condescend now and then, to converse familiarly with us," noted the young midshipman, James Trevenen. "But it was only for the time, as soon as we entered the ships, he became again the despot."

A day or two later, Cook returned to Friendly Cove, in search of grass to feed the few sheep and goats that still survived on board. He was amazed to discover that he must buy the grass from its owners — something that might have amazed him less had he tried to acquire grass from English owners. "I have no were met with Indians who had such high notions of every thing the Country produced being their exclusive property," he exclaimed.

Almost a month after the ships arrived at Nootka, the repairs were complete, the remasting and rerigging finished, the tools and observatories loaded back on board. On April 26, as the mercury in the barometer fell and a thick haze warned of approaching storms, Cook determined to be gone. Wrote Trevenen, "It was Cook's constant maxim & practice never to wait in port for a fair wind but to go to Sea & look for one," and, in a burst of patriotism, "it is much more the characteristic of English seamen than of any others." The Dutch sea captain, claimed Trevenen, never stirs out of port until the weather settles; the Englishman may lose by his brashness, but he makes three voyages to the Dutchman's two — if, the cautious reader must add, he is not drowned in the process.

At noon on April 26, the wind and tide turned, and all hands manned the boats' oars to tow the ships out of Resolution Cove into the sound. The Nootka paddled alongside; some stayed as guests aboard the *Resolution* until it had reached the head of the sound. Cook presented the Nootkan chief who stayed aboard with a present; the chief presented Cook with a sea otter skin. Not wanting to be outdone, Cook gave another present. The chief responded with an otter-skin cloak. Cook ended the exchange with a new brass-hilted broadsword, and everyone was content.

The Nootka returned to their canoes and watched the ships out of the sound. A storm blew up, turning the sky so dark that the sailors "could not see the length of the Ship." With his ships threatened by the storm, Cook sailed out of danger, well clear of the coast, then turned northwest, paralleling, he believed, the coastline he could not see. The gale blew for a day and a half, and the *Resolution* sprang a leak that at first caused serious concern. But the pumps were equal to the task of keeping the ship dry. A second gale blew up on April 30, and Cook had to give up on one of his goals: disproving the existence of the strait that Admiral de Fonte had claimed existed at 53° north latitude. It would have been "imprudent to sail toward land given the weather, or lose the wind by waiting for better conditions." Impatient now to reach his goal of 60° north, Cook sailed out of sight of land west of the Queen Charlotte Islands, sighted by Perez, and Prince of Wales Island, seen by Russian explorer Aleksei Chirikov: catching sight of the coast again when he reached the westward-trending Alaskan Peninsula on May 2.

Now began one of the most frustrating months of Cook's years of exploring. It is one thing to sail across open ocean, thereby disproving the existence of a great body of land. It is another, given the dangers of wind and weather close to the coast and the drawbacks of sail, to sail along a large body of land, looking for a strait or river or gulf that may or may not exist. Yet his previous journeys had taught him that the attempt must be made. "Was it not," he wrote in his journal of the second voyage, "for the Pleasure which Naturly results to a man from his being the first discoverer even was it nothing more than Sand and Shoals this kind of service would be insupportable especially in distant parts like this, Short of Provisions & almost every other necessary. People will hardly admit of a man leaving a coast unexplored he has once discover'd, if dangers are his excuse he is then charged with timerousness & want of Perseverance, & at once pronounced the most unfit man in the world to be employed as a discoverer, if on the other hand he boldly encounters all the dangers & obstacles he meets with & is unfortunate enough not to succeed he is then charged with Temerity & perhaps want of conduct."

Prematurely aged by the hardships he had encountered and lacking the verve of a younger man, Cook continued on, indecisive and weary, seeking a harbour where they might repair the leak to the *Resolution*. He found his refuge on the Alaskan Peninsula, in Prince William Sound, and ordered the ship heeled over. The men ripped off the sheathing — only

Yellow mimulus clings to sea-washed rocks. The characteristics that allow mimulus to survive in the marine environment — hardiness, ability to weather Pacific storms and resistance to salt — must have been shared by the early mariners as well.

to find the seams open and the oakum caulking completely rotted away. The carpenters filled the seams with rope while the rest of the crew filled the casks with fresh water and communicated as best they could with curious natives who approached the ships.

The ship repaired, he followed in the wake of Bering and Chirikov. Comparing what he saw to what the Russian charts suggested, Cook sought a new course: he found a "fine opening," but a gale from the west held them outside its mouth. Should he wait? Should he go on? The winds eased, and he tacked into the inlet, hopeful that it might be an entrance leading at the least to the Bering Sea, at the best to a passage northeast. Three hundred kilometres up the inlet, Cook decided this could not be a passage: the water was now fresh, not salt, and it must therefore be a river. The river might one day prove of importance, but to him, it was just a waste of precious time: by exploring it farther, he could only delay and perhaps doom his explorations northwards. But, he mused, had he not traced its course, many might have said he had missed the northwest passage.

Disappointed, Cook now sailed five hundred kilometres along the Alaskan Peninsula, then around the Aleutians, through Norton Sound, and across Bering Strait, anchoring near the coast of Siberia. He then commanded his ships north, where they spent until mid-August seeking a passage. On August 17, a solid wall of pack ice barred their way. For a week, they sought a way through, casting east and west, but found no entry. Cook came to two conclusions as the week wore on.

Those who insisted that a northwest passage must exist drew support from their contention that sea water did not freeze: an ice-free passage north of North America was, therefore, almost a certainty. But Cook now decided these scientists were wrong: the pack ice he faced was the product of more than one year, so sea water must freeze. "There is always a remaining store [of Arctic ice]," he stated. Impatient with those who said otherwise without ever having seen a polar sea, he wrote that "none who has been on the spot will deny and none but Closet Studdying Philosiphers will dispute."

He also decided it was time to turn south, to return the following year to northern seas. "I did not think it consistent with prudence to make further attempts to find a passage this year in any direction so little was the prospect of succeeding," he wrote. Instead, he would take his ships to look for wood and water, and to consider how and where to spend the winter. Jason King, second lieutenant on the *Resolution*, concurred: "Those who have been amongst Ice in the dread of being enclosed in it, & in so late in a season can be the best judge of the joy that this news gave."

The ships turned back to the Aleutians, where the crews met Russian traders who filled in or corrected charts for Cook. They left the coast for the season on October 24. An uneventful passage brought them back to Hawaii on November 26.

The Hawaiians welcomed them back with fruit, vegetables and pigs. At their next stop on the islands, fifteen hundred canoes with nine thousand Hawaiians aboard, and many more on surfboards, surrounded

the ships. Wrote Cook in his journals, "few . . . now lamented our having failed in our endeavour to find a northward passage homeward last summer. To this disappointment we owed our having it in our power to revisit the Sandwich Isles, and to enrich our voyage with a discovery which, though the last, seemed in every respect, to be the most important that had hitherto been made by Europeans throughout the extent of the Pacific Ocean." Cook set up his observatories and tents, and prepared for a happy stay.

It was not to be. Whether through misunderstanding, latent hostility or other cause, relations were soon strained between the English sailors and the Hawaiians, who

The sea otter's luxuriant coat allows it to survive in the frigid waters of the Pacific. Cook's men brought pelts to Asia on their voyage home, starting a "fur rush" that eventually almost wiped out the abundant populations of sea otter on the coast.

soon grew weary of these guests who did not leave. Thefts occurred; fights broke out. On February 14, two and a half months after he arrived in Hawaii, Cook found himself surrounded by angry Hawaiians on shore. Shouts and shots were exchanged. Cook turned to wave the boats in, to help his outnumbered men. As he turned, a high priest struck him down with a club. In seconds, others had stabbed him. The greatest navigator of the eighteenth century

Cook was a man of the sea. His work charting coastlines around the world laid the foundations for the explorations of the following century.

died on the beach at Kavarua, aged fifty, half a globe away from home.

His death ended neither the expedition nor the growth of his reputation. Cook's remains were lowered into the sea. Clerke took the two ships north the following season, but to no avail, and Clerke himself died on the way south, of tuberculosis. With both commanders dead, the ships turned homewards. They arrived in England on October 4, 1780, four years and three months after they set sail.

The news of Cook's death reached England, via letters from Siberia, ten months before the ships came home. "Poor Cook is truly a great loss to the Universe," wrote one commentator, and the king was said to have shed tears when he heard the news.

Cook's reputation lived on and grew. Never a romantic, always a practical man of the sea, Cook had filled in the map of the world's oceans to a degree never before, and never since, achieved by one man. His work would underlie the journeys of the next century.

Ironically, it was not this work of chart-making that had the greatest impact on the northwest coast. The sailors on the *Resolution*, knowing they were headed for frigid Arctic waters, traded assiduously for sea otter furs. The ships went home by way of Canton; in that Chinese port, the crew quickly learned that their furs, worn and dirty though they might be, could fetch a fine price. One midshipman had traded the rim of a broken buckle for a sea otter pelt; that pelt brought him three hundred dollars in China, enough "for his own necessities [and] silk gowns, fans, tea and other articles," which he took home as presents

for his sisters and his friends.

Once the ships returned to England, the word quickly spread. Within five years, ships sailing under the British flag came to Nootka to obtain sea otter pelts. By 1789, British and American ships both were sail-

ing from the coast, laden with the furs. Cook's men, all unwitting, had started a trade that would have great repercussions for the northwest coast. The men who sought the pelts were driven by desire for wealth, not by any scientific curiosity, and their treatment of the natives grew steadily worse over the decades. And so valued were sea otter skins in China that traders for the next century scoured the coast seeking them, and, in the end, almost exterminated the silky-pelted sea beasts.

George Vancouver: A Man Haughty and Proud

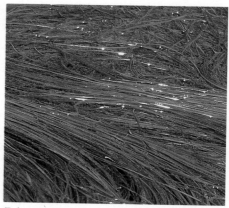

Eelgrass in the tide pools found along the outer coast of Vancouver Island and elsewhere along Vancouver's route conceals edible marine life, from mussels and algae to octopi and small fish trapped by the outgoing tide.

Through the long days of the Antarctic summer of 1773-4, HMS *Resolution* shivered south. Though the freezing damp ate at their bones, the crew persevered, eager for the honour of sailing farther south than any man had ever before recorded. When James Cook finally gave the order to come about, his way blocked by an impenetrable field of ice, a sixteen-year-old midshipman wriggled out to the end of the bowsprit, waved his cap in the air and shouted, *"Ne plus ultra!"* — "No man farther!"

Two years later, that same midshipman, George Vancouver, sailed aboard the *Discovery*, Cook's companion ship on his third and fatal voyage. The day before

Cook's death, Vancouver piled aboard the *Discovery*'s cutter with other crew members, pursuing Hawaiian natives who had snatched tools from the ship. Thomas Edgar, the master of the *Resolution*, seized hold of the canoe near shore. The natives

Cape Mudge on Quadra Island. On his first command, George Vancouver was directed to investigate and chart the coast and islands of the northeast Pacific, seeking still a northeast passage.

"At should seem, that the reign of George the Third had been reserved by the Great Disposer of all things, for the glorious task of establishing the grand key-stone to that expansive arch, over which the arts and sciences should pass to the furthermost corners of the earth." — From Vancouver's introduction to his journal.

resisted; stones flew; the cutter grounded in the shallows. The crew swam to a nearby rock, where one of the Hawaiians swung a broken oar at Edgar. Vancouver pushed in front and took the blow intended for his superior officer. He slumped to the ground and someone snatched his cap and fled with it. A chief friendly to Cook's men intervened, and the crew were able to rescue Vancouver. The next day, Cook was not as lucky.

George Vancouver was just twenty years old when Cook was killed, and already a seasoned seaman. Born of a monied English family, he joined the navy when he was fifteen, and soon became a midshipman, in training for an officer's position. He served on Cook's second and third expedition, was commissioned as a lieutenant on his return to England, then worked the Caribbean, in war and peace, for almost ten years. Assigned as second-in-command to an expedition bound for the northwest coast of America, he was promoted to captain when the expedition was delayed and the original captain sent to the Caribbean. By then, he had gained a reputation as an excellent seaman and geographer, but an officer harsh and irascible even by the standards of the eighteenth-century British navy.

HMS *Discovery*, Vancouver in command, sailed from England with her companion ship *Chatham* on April 1, 1791. The Admiralty had assigned Vancouver three tasks: to explore those parts of the North Pacific coast still uncharted, to find a northwest passage or put to rest the idea of its existence, and to oversee the return of British territory and property taken over by the Spanish at Nootka. The expedition followed

a by-now familiar route: to Capetown, thence across the Indian Ocean to Australia, to New Zealand, and into the South Pacific. After a series of delays caused by the need to repair the ships, to allow the sailors to recover from illnesses, or simply to take on supplies, the *Discovery* and the *Chatham* weighed anchor and sailed from the Hawaiian Islands for the northwest coast in mid-March of 1792.

Vancouver's voyage across the Pacific was as uneventful as Cook's, though Archibald Menzies, assistant surgeon and botanist on board the *Discovery* and no respecter of naval tradition, shot a large brown albatross. Gales were succeeded by fair weather, fair weather by wind. On April 18, one year and eighteen days after the *Discovery* weighed anchor and sailed from home, the lookout sighted the coast of America, revealed and obscured through heavy slanting rain and shifting fog. The ships turned north near present-day Mendocino, California, and sailed along a "verdant, agreeable coast."

The Admiralty had instructed Vancouver to acquire "accurate information with respect to the nature and extent of any water-communication which may tend, in any considerable degree, to facilitate an intercourse for the purposes of commerce between the northwest coast, and the countries upon the other side of the continent which are inhabited or occupied by His Majesty's subjects." Vancouver was further instructed to chart the general line of the coast, for even if no such passage existed, "it would be of great importance if it should be found that, by means of any considerable inlets of the sea, or even large rivers, communicating with the lakes in the interior of the continent, such intercourse could be established.'' For somehow, despite the skepticism of Cook and the maps and explorations by the sailors of four nations, belief in the ''discoveries'' of de Fuca and de Fonte still survived. Surely, said the believers, there must be some substance to the shadowy claims of a great inlet that led to the Atlantic, or a River of Kings that slashed deep into the continent.

Vancouver was more hard-headed. He would make, he wrote, ''the history of our transactions in the north west coast of America, as conclusive as possible, against all speculative opinion respecting the existence of a hyperborean or mediterranean ocean within the limits of our survey.''

Now within sight of the coast, he set to his task. Bedevilled, like any modern traveller, by fog and haze that hid the coast, Vancouver sailed a league offshore, looking for and failing to find a harbour. North of 46 degrees latitude, he remarked a sandy beach made inaccessible by breakers that extended far into the sea. He sailed on, past the bar at the mouth of the Columbia River. Noted Thomas Manby, a midshipman on the *Discovery*: ''a continued roll of breakers lay right across its entrance, it may [be] from a River and perhaps admissible at certain periods. We had it not in our power to loiter away any time on it at present, intending to inspect it farther on a future day.'' Vancouver had no great interest in rivers the ship could not enter.

A few days later, the crew spotted a sail; it was ''a very great novelty,'' noted Vancouver, ''not having seen any vessel but our consort in the last eight months.'' The American ship *Columbia*, under the command of Robert Gray, drew alongside, and the two captains exchanged pleasantries and information. British trader and renegade John Meares had reported that Gray had sailed through Juan de Fuca's supposed strait. No indeed, said Gray: he had penetrated only about eighty kilometres up the waterway. Manby was amused by the discrepancy. Quite probably, he commented in a letter, Gray had played a small joke on the credulous Meares, then sailed away from Nootka, smiling.

The *Discovery* and the *Chatham* turned east into the strait, then spent a month exploring the north coast of the Olympic Peninsula and the inlets between the mainland and the peninsula. Vancouver and his officers charted each ripple of the shore, naming bays, islands and sounds for crew members, friends and Lords of the Admiralty with easy impartiality: thus, Puget Sound and Whidbey Island were named for crew, Port Townsend and Mount Rainier for friends, and Hood Canal for the member of the Admiralty board who had signed Vancouver's orders.

In June, the expedition turned north again. Vancouver realized by now that he could not make best progress in the sailing ships. Instead, he provisioned the ships' boats, and split up his crews, sending men out in each boat to row along and chart portions of the coastline, a method of operating he was to use for the rest of the voyage. He went aboard the yawl, with Puget aboard the launch, north along the mainland coast. He noted two openings between Point Roberts and Point Grey (the two arms of the Fraser River), ''to approach which all our endeavours were exerted to no purpose.'' The crew worked the oars for ten and a half hours that day, then

''*The King having judged it expedient that an expedition should be immediately undertaken for acquiring a more complete knowledge than has yet been obtained; you are, in pursuance of His Majesty's pleasure . . . to repair to the north-west coast of America.''* — From the Admiralty's instructions to George Vancouver, 1790.

found little rest that night: forced out into mid-channel by the shoals, they could find nowhere to land on the gulf's western shore, and had to sleep in their boats, probably anchored alongside Gabriola Island.

The next day, they tried again to investigate the eastern shore, but a large, swampy flat ahead barred their way. Vancouver's lieutenant, Peter Puget, suspected that the two distant openings must be the mouths of rivers, but Vancouver gave up any attempt to enter them, since they could "be navigable only to canoes, as the shoal continues along the coast to the distance of seven or eight miles from the shore, on which were lodged, and especially before these openings, logs of wood and stumps of trees innumerable." This, he decided, could be no large river communicating with lakes in the interior of the continent.

The men now rowed and sailed east around Point Grey, through the First Narrows, and into what would one day be the inner harbour of the great city named for Vancouver. A flotilla of Indian canoes accompanied them, but Vancouver was

"The land which interrupted the horizon . . . was bounded by a ridge of snowy mountains, appearing to lie nearly in a north and south direction, on which mount Baker rose conspicuously; remarkable for its height, and the snowy mountains that stretch from its base to the north and south." — May 2, 1792

The volcanic cone of dormant Mount Baker dominates the Lower Mainland area skyline. Vancouver named it after one of his officers.

Savary Island was named by Vancouver, as the flotilla of two British and two Spanish vessels sailed between the mainland and the small island, near this spot.

determined not to trust their occupants. If they had seemed unfriendly, Vancouver would undoubtedly have been edgy. Since they expressed "cordiality and respect," Vancouver was definitely wary, for "this sort of conduct always created a degree of suspicion." Vancouver was always concerned when he saw the natives of any place talking together, lest the conversation indicate some hostile plan, though, he wrote, in fact he had never noticed afterward "any alteration of their friendly disposition."

The boats continued up Burrard Inlet to the entrance to Indian Arm, where the men camped overnight — some of them damply, not having considered the incoming tide when they chose to sleep on the beach instead of in the boats. They returned down the inlet and rowed north into a region that intimidated Vancouver not a little. "The low fertile shores we had been accustomed to see . . . here no longer existed," he wrote in mid-June. "Their place was now occupied by the base of the stupendous snowy barrier, thinly wooded and rising from the sea abruptly to the clouds, from whose frigid summit, the dissolving snow in foaming torrents rushed down the sides and chasms of its rugged surface, exhibiting altogether a sublime, though gloomy spectacle. . . . Not a bird, nor living creature was to be seen, and the roaring of falling cataracts in every direction precluded their being heard, had any been in our neighbourhood." Farther north they went, into a region he dubbed dreary and comfortless, gloomy and unproductive.

Other crew members were equally overpowered by their surroundings. Menzies, ever the author of purple prose, wrote on

"We seemed now to have forsaken the main direction of the gulf, being on every side encompassed by islands and small rocky islets; some lying along the continental shore, others confusedly scattered, of different forms and dimensions. . . . Through this very unpleasant navigation we sailed. . . ." — June 25, 1792

The arbutus tree characterizes the southern British Columbia coastline charted by Vancouver.

The grassy bluffs around Dinner Rock, just south of Powell River, are brightened in springtime by flowering Saskatoon bushes, chocolate lilies and blue camas. Vancouver's and Quadra's ships had been travelling together, but near here the Spanish fell behind, unable to keep pace with the larger, faster British ships.

June 23 about Jervis Inlet: "In going up the Arm they here and there passed immense Cascades rushing down from the summits of high Precipices & dashing headlong down chasms against projecting Rocks and Cliffs with a furious wildness that beggard all description. Curiosity led them [the crew of one boat] to approach one of the largest where it pourd its foaming pondrous stream over high rugged cliffs & precipices into the fretted Sea with such stunning noise & rapidity of motion that they could not look up to its sourse without being affected with giddiness nor contemplate its romantic wildness without a mixture of awe and admiration."

Almost out of food after ten days spent rowing on one week's provisions, the seamen turned their boats back towards the main ships. The boat crews had rowed and sailed more than five hundred kilometres in eleven days, an average of forty-five kilometres a day. Vancouver and Puget travelled ahead in the pinnace, Manby behind in the launch. On their way back to the ship, the two were separated, and Manby's crew returned late to the ship, after suffering from a violent bout of shellfish poisoning, then going three days with only the food they could shoot, and travelling without the benefit of a compass. Delighted to have found his way back to the ship, Manby was dismayed and disgusted when Vancouver delivered a highly critical harangue. It was, wrote Manby, "a salutation I can never forget, and his language I will never forgive, unless he withdraws his words by a satisfactory apology."

Vancouver may have been made more irritable by the "no small degree of mortification" he experienced when he came upon the *Mexicana* and the *Sutil*, two Spanish ships under the command of Dionisio Alcala Galiano and Cayetano Valdes, exploring the strait and the shores. Swallowing his humiliation that the Spanish had already visited and charted these waters some distance beyond where he had been, Vancouver suggested the four ships should continue together, sharing their task.

They anchored next in Teakerne Arm, a location that Vancouver disliked heartily. "Our residence here was truly forlorn. An awful silence pervaded the gloomy forests, whilst animated nature seemed to have deserted the neighbouring country, whose soil afforded only a few small onions, some samphire, and here and there bushes bearing a scanty crop of indifferent berries. Nor was the sea more favourable to our wants, the steep rocky shores prevented the use of the seine, and not a fish at the bottom could be tempted to take the hook."

Depressed, dispirited, or simply disenchanted by the countryside, Vancouver named his next anchorage Desolation Sound. Finding the country to be completely lacking in beauty, recreational opportunities, or even a good food supply, Vancouver's only solace lay in the Spanish ships; he wrote, "Our time would have passed infinitely more heavily, had it not been relieved by the agreeable society of our Spanish friends."

He was cheered, however, by the return of Johnstone's party at two in the morning on July 12, with the news that they had found a passage leading to the northwest, to the Pacific Ocean. That same day, the faster British ships left the Spaniards

*The inlet north of present-day Powell River was not one of Vancouver's favourite places.
Although contemporary sailors come from around the world to experience its warm waters,
grand views and abundant marine life, the great surveyor named it Desolation Sound.*

behind, and the *Discovery* and the *Chatham* continued on alone. They anchored off Cape Mudge, on Quadra Island, and Vancouver, Menzies and some of the other officers went ashore after dinner. Vancouver was impressed by the Kwakiutl native village, "the houses of which were built after the fashion of Nootka.... The spot where it was erected appeared to be well chosen to insure its protection; the steep loose sandy precipice secured it in front, and its rear was defended by a deep chasm in the rocks; beyond these was a thick and nearly impenetrable forest: so that the only means of access was the narrow path we had ascended, which could be easily maintained against very superior numbers."

The *Discovery* and the *Chatham* sailed north, with the men dispatched in the small boats to explore and chart each cove and inlet. As he sailed north, Vancouver named Johnstone Strait, Bute Inlet, Loughborough Inlet, and a hundred other places.

At daybreak on August 6, calm overtook the ships, and thick fog enshrouded the *Discovery*, "so that [they] were left to the mercy of the currents, in a situation that could not fail to occasion the most anxious solicitude." The fog lifted, a breeze sprang up — and the ship immediately went aground on rocks in Richards Channel, opposite the northern end of Vancouver Island. The stream anchor was carried out, and the men tried to heave the ship off the rocks; the men of the *Chatham*'s boats bent to their oars. But the *Discovery* was not to be moved by brute force. Vancouver's men took down the sails and masts, shored up the ship with spare masts and spars, and threw overboard fuel and ballast. The *Discovery* swung hard with the

"This afforded not a single prospect that was pleasing to the eye, the smallest recreation on shore, nor animal or vegetable food, excepting a very scanty proportion of those eatables ... of which the adjacent country was soon exhausted, after our arrival." — July 5, 1792

Vancouver's journals of his voyage along the inside of Vancouver Island contain entries about whales and other marine life. Johnstone Strait, named by Vancouver for the officer who first examined this channel, is today one of the best places in the world to see orcas, or killer whales.

receding tide, heeling over so that her starboard main chains were within a few centimetres of the sea. "Happily," wrote Vancouver, ". . . there was not the slightest swell or agitation . . . [otherwise] nothing short of immediate and inevitable destruction presented itself," until "toward the latter part of the ebb tide . . . more than one half the ship was supported by such a sufficient body of water, as in a great measure, to relieve us from the painful anxiety that so distressing a circumstance necessarily occasioned." The ship righted itself, miraculously without any serious injury, and the voyage continued.

Scant hours later, the *Chatham* went aground. A thick fog hid the ship from the men aboard the *Discovery*, but the tide drifted the *Chatham* off the rocks, and she soon caught up with her sister ship. The

two ships continued northward, and the men bent to the oars of the five ships' boats again, charting the bays and inlets that slashed into the coast. Fog, gales and rain plagued their explorations, but they were cheered by the sight of a trading ship flying the British flag. The captain of the *Venus*, sailing out of Bengal, informed them that their supply ship, the *Daedalus*, was waiting for them at Nootka.

It was now mid-August. The weather had turned cold and sullen, and Vancouver decided it was time to sail for Nootka, where he could complete the diplomatic business with which he had been entrusted. The men greeted his decision with pleasure. "The weather," wrote Menzies, "was now become so cold wet and uncomfortable that the men were no longer able to endure the fatiguing hardships of distant excursions in open boats exposed to the cold rigorous blasts of a high northern situation with high, dreary snowy mountains on every side, performing toilsome labour on their oars in the days, & alternately watching for their own safety at night, with no other couch to repose upon than the cold stony beach or the wet mossy Turf in damp woody situations, without having shelter sufficient to screen them from the inclemency of boisterous weather, & enduring at times the tormenting pangs of both hunger and thirst, yet on every occasion struggling who should be the most forward in executing the orders of their superiors to accomplish the general interest of the voyage." On he writes, a long encomium to the "persevering integrity & manly steadiness" of officers and men.

Sailing west, then south, Vancouver proved beyond doubt that the shores he had

"They here and there passed immense Cascades rushing down from the Summits of high precipices & dashing headlong down chasms against projecting Rocks and Cliffs with a furious wildness that beggard all description." — From the diary of Archibald Menzies.

charted were of both mainland and a large island, on which Nootka lay. On August 28, he arrived at Friendly Cove, in Nootka Sound. In the years since Cook's visit, traders from Britain, the United States, Russia and Spain had been active on the coast; most made their base at Nootka. In 1789, the Spanish commander at Nootka had seized two ships that flew the British flag and sent them under guard to Spanish settlements in Mexico. John Meares, part owner of the ships, appealed to the British government for satisfaction; war between Britain and Spain seemed certain. But the crisis passed without a shot being fired, and Spain agreed to restore British territory at Nootka to Britain, and to compensate Britain for the property seized. Vancouver

Despite its drawbacks, the wet coastal climate of British Columbia provided the expedition with a luxury — unlimited fresh water. Waterfalls such as this one along the Inside Passage are common on the coast.

An abalone shell in the sands of Cape Scott. From here, Vancouver continued south to Nootka Sound, completing his circumnavigation of Vancouver Island. At Nootka, where he again met Quadra, Vancouver commemorated their friendship by naming the island the "Island of Quadra and Vancouver."

was charged with supervising the return of British territory at Nootka.

When Vancouver and his ships arrived, the Spanish governor, Juan Francisco de la Bodega y Quadra, fired a thirteen-gun salute to welcome them; Vancouver fired one in return. The Spanish officers on shore came aboard for a polite breakfast; Vancouver and his officers went to dinner ashore. Oddly, considering his diplomatic mission, Vancouver had no one aboard who could speak and translate Spanish; fortunately, a young gentleman aboard the *Daedalus* could do so, and volunteered to act as translator.

In language elegant, diplomatic, but firm, Bodega y Quadra informed Vancouver that he could not return all of Nootka to Britain. He was more than willing, he said, to return the land where Meares had built his ship, together with whatever buildings remained, but that land was just a small triangle. Spain was legitimately in possession of, and would remain in possession of, the rest of the area. Bodega y Quadra would remove himself and his men to another settlement if Vancouver insisted, but he could not, would not, give up Spain's territorial claims.

While Vancouver could not accept Bodega y Quadra's terms, he could accept his hospitality. Vancouver and his officers went ashore almost every night, to dine on silver plate changed for each of the five dinner courses, with silver cutlery, and all due pomp and ceremony. Bodega y Quadra had gardens full of vegetables and fruit; beef, pork, chicken and fresh salmon were served at his table. He had imported, at great personal expense, brandy and vintage wine, dried fruit and cheese and

pickles. For men at sea for more than a year and more than tired of wormy salt pork and bland hardtack, the delights of the Spanish table were seductive.

For Vancouver, they were a relief from life aboard ship. Though his men might respect Vancouver's seamanship and scientific knowledge, they did not love him. No shipmate, in letter or diary, expresses affection or friendship for the captain of the *Discovery*. Hours spent with Bodega y Quadra, who was unfailingly respectful and friendly, restored Vancouver's good humour. Vancouver and Quadra went visiting up Tahsis Inlet together; when Quadra suggested it would be fitting to "commemorate our meeting and the very friendly intercourse that had taken place and subsisted between us" by naming some geographic feature for them both, Vancouver was delighted to comply: he named the island he had just circumnavigated the Island of Quadra and Vancouver, "with which compliment he [Quadra] seemed highly pleased."

Beyond his diplomatic depth, Vancouver decided to refer the territorial dispute back

"*About cape Scot the land is composed of hills of moderate height, though to the south-eastward it soon becomes very mountainous, and at the distance of three to four leagues appeared to be much broken and to form many inlets.*" — *August 25, 1792*

to London. He must have had some sense that he had been outmaneuvred, perhaps even compromised by his friendship, for, he wrote, "I acted to the best of my judgement. Should I be so unfortunate, however, as to incur any censure, I must rely on the candor of my country to do me the justice of attributing whatever improprieties I may appear to have committed to the true and only cause; to a want of sufficient diplomatic skill, which a life wholly devoted to my profession had denied me the opportunity of acquiring."

Bodega y Quadra now sailed for San Blas, in Mexico; not long after, deeply in debt for the supplies he had ordered so lavishly for the establishment at Nootka, he died.

With winter approaching, the *Discovery*, the *Chatham* and the *Daedalus* hauled out of Friendly Cove on October 12, with Vancouver bound south for San Francisco and the other Spanish settlements along the coast. In November, he turned west again, for the Hawaiian Islands, where he spent a relatively uneventful winter. The following March, of 1793, he sailed again for the northwest coast of America.

On the voyage, Vancouver wrote of the diet aboard ship, his astronomical observations, the state of the masts and sails, the direction of the winds. His officers, meanwhile, were writing about him. Almost from the beginning of the voyage, Vancouver had made himself unpopular with his officers and men. Beset by the problems of command, perhaps worn down by ill health, perhaps suffering from the illness diagnosed by twentieth-century historians as a thyroid complaint, since early in the trip Vancouver had displayed fits of violent temper, spurts of immense energy and advancing paranoia. He had forbidden his midshipmen to go ashore in Tahiti; he had flogged Thomas Pitt, a midshipman, several times, though flogging someone of noble family was a rarity in the navy. He had threatened to burn houses and canoes in a Tahitian village unless some stolen linen was restored. He had taken the fires that burned routinely on the hills of the Hawaiian islands for signals for war; he believed some of the Hawaiians were trying to drown him and his men. At times, in bad weather, he called for all hands on deck; when the wind was fair, he might keep them tacking the ship, working the men hard. "As they would not work when there was Occasion, they should when there was not," he told his officers. In June of 1793, Manby wrote that no good fellowship existed on board the *Discovery*, "owing to the conduct of our commander-in-chief who is grown Haughty, Proud and Insolent, which has kept himself and Officers in a continual state of wrangling during the whole of the voyage."

By his decisions, wrote one officer, Vancouver had rendered himself universally obnoxious; he was particularly harsh towards his "poor kick'd about, abused, despised Midshipmen." The crew on the *Chatham*, the journalists noted, were much better treated.

But no one argued Vancouver's skills as a surveyor. Though various difficulties delayed Vancouver's return to Nootka until late May and limited his season's surveying to just four months instead of five, through the summer of 1793, the crews of the *Discovery* and the *Chatham* explored each curve and indentation between the tip

of Vancouver Island and the Alaska Panhandle. Vancouver had the ships anchor in seven successive harbours up the coast, then dispatched the small boats and the men who rowed them to chart the coastline.

Vancouver had learned from last year's experience; over the winter, he had his men make awnings and canopies to protect the boats from the weather. Each now contained a large tent with a painted cloth floor, and painted canvas bags for provisions and clothing. Each now carried enough wheat flour and portable soup — a sort of meat bouillon — to provide the crew with two hot meals a day, and the

officer in charge had spirits to be issued at his discretion. Beyond this, the men could fish and hunt: on the eve of the King's birthday, one boat crew was able to feast on "Bear Steaks, stewd Eagle, and roasted Muscles, with as much glee as a City Alderman attacks his Venison."

Exploring and charting from the boats was still laborious, tedious work. As anyone who has sailed the Inside Passage from Howe Sound to Alaska can testify, the twists and turnings of the coastline are myriad, the bays, coves, inlets, channels and straits countless. On one twenty-three-day expedition away from the ships, the boat crews covered more than eleven hundred

This typical coastal scene near Prince Rupert — morning mist with light rain — is close to the mouth of the Skeena River, one of the three great rivers Vancouver passed by.

kilometres, rowing almost all the way, yet advancing the map of the continental shoreline just a hundred kilometres north.

Whether because he was in ill health — the most likely explanation — or because he was weary of the process, Vancouver himself commanded just two of the boat expeditions, one of ten days and the second of twenty-three. On the first, he explored Fisher, Dean and Return channels, meeting Bella Bella and Bella Coola Indians on the way. He was no more impressed with the country than he had been the previous year, with the "rough, rainy and unpleasant weather" combined with steep-sided inlets that kept them from camping ashore. He recorded in punctilious detail the tides, the weather, the appearance of the countryside and the manners of the natives he met. He then returned to the ship, and after another day

or two of making astronomical observations, sailed north again. At their next anchorage, the small boats of the *Chatham* returned with distressing news. "Several of the crew who had eaten of the muscles," Vancouver recorded, "were seized with a numbness about their faces and their extremities; their whole bodies were very shortly affected with the same manner." The crew had tried various remedies — working up a sweat by vigorous rowing, drinking large amounts of warm water — but, despite their efforts, two of the men died. Vancouver named the spot where the shellfish were taken Poison Cove and promptly banned the eating of mussels for the rest of the voyage.

Vancouver proceeded north from anchorage to anchorage, dispatching the men in the boats to explore the surrounding land and water. Late in July, the ships reached Observatory Inlet, where the *Discovery* anchored and Vancouver set up his tents, observatory, chronometers and instruments on shore. He sent two officers off in charge of two small boats; Vancouver set off in another for what would be a twenty-three-day exploration of the inlet and Portland and Pearse canals.

On the night of July 25, they camped by the side of Hastings Inlet. "Although a situation for our tents was fixed upon amongst the pine trees, at least twenty feet above the surface of the water at our landing," wrote Vancouver, "yet . . . it flowed into the tents, and we were obliged to retire to our boats."

Worse was to come. All through his explorations of the northwest coast, Vancouver's men and the natives — Nootka, Kwakiutl, Bella Bella, Bella Coola, Haida —

Steller's and California sea lions are found along the coast of Vancouver Island. They were probably quite impervious to Vancouver's men, whose powerless boats would not be able to safely approach the rocky islets where the sea lions haul out.

had got on well together, communicating and trading with civility and even friendship. Now, almost at what would be the border between British Columbia and the Alaska Panhandle, the men encountered a party of natives who were disdainful and indifferent; Vancouver feared they would attack. The dispute, whatever its nature, was resolved, but relations between the two groups were edgy and uncertain for the next few days.

Relations between seamen and natives continued to be sour, and, in mid-August, a group of Tlingit attacked a boat carrying Vancouver along the shore. Did the Tlingit

"Our sails were scarcely set when the wind became variable; and soon after mid-day partial fogs and a clear atmosphere succeeded each other in every direction." — August 8, 1792

Today sailors have the benefit of sophisticated weather tracking and communications equipment. Vancouver relied solely on barometers and intuition when confronted with towering cumulus clouds such as these.

resent what they saw as an invasion of their territory? Had they been badly treated by other trading parties, and grown wary of intruders? Did they view the Europeans as, no more and no less, the equivalent of a rival native group? Vancouver did not know and, lacking journals for posterity, the Tlingit did not say. Whatever the reason for the encounter, it saddened Vancouver. Though, like most Europeans of his time, he saw North American natives — and, indeed, all the natives he had encountered on his travels — as uncivilized and inferior beings, he had no desire to harm them.

Though his instructions commanded him to explore any river that might lead far inland, he dismissed the mouths of the Skeena and Nass as negligible, for they were "too insignificant to be dignified by the name of rivers and in truth scarcely deserve the appellation of rivulets." His officers were less convinced: Puget wanted to explore the Skeena, and Menzies speculated that the Nass might lead to a chain of lakes and rivers, a natural communication channel for the fur trade from Canada or Hudson Bay.

The ships sailed on north, through the intricacies of the panhandle coastline, to "latitude 56 degrees, 2 minutes." This was, Vancouver declared, the point at which all of de Fuca's and de Fonte's supposed discoveries could be discredited once and for all; he called it Cape Decision. "Had any river or opening in the coast existed near either the 43d or 53d parallel of north latitude, the plausible system that has been erected [hypotheses of a northwest passage] would most likely have been deemed perfect; but unfortunately for the ingenuity of its *hypothetical projectors*, our *practical labours* have thus far made it totter." Convinced he had finished his most important task, that of proving or disproving the existence of a passage in these latitudes, he turned southward in late September, bound for Nootka, San Francisco, San Diego, and Hawaii.

It was his last visit to Hawaii. He arrived in early January and left again in mid-March, much more impressed by the hospitality of the Hawaiians than by the behaviour of the Spanish governor in California, who had insulted and been rude to Vancouver and his officers. Vancouver

The southern end of Vancouver Island, with its onshore winds, fickle weather, tricky currents and pounding surf, can be a mariner's nightmare even with modern-day technology and charts, making Vancouver's achievements even more impressive.

He had hoped, he wrote, to finish his journey without firing a shot in anger. Now he had done so, and several Tlingit were killed or injured.

He returned to the *Discovery* and *Chatham*, where he recorded the discoveries made by the men in the other boats.

sent three of his midshipmen home with the *Daedalus*; among them was Thomas Pitt, now the Baron Camelford, whom Vancouver could no longer tolerate aboard his ship.

Vancouver also accomplished what he considered a great diplomatic coup: the cession of the islands by their leaders to Britain. Coup though it was, it had no immediate results, since no one but Vancouver and his crews were aware of it.

The next spring, Vancouver returned once more to the northwest coast, resuming the task of charting the shoreline and adjacent islands. By August, they were working their way up Cook's Inlet, in Alaska, with the cabin temperature down to fourteen degrees below zero Celsius and ice chunks running in the tides. On his last venture in the boats, Vancouver spent eighteen days surveying from Cape Decision to Port Conclusion, near the southern end of Baranoff Island. On August 18, 1794, he declared his work completed. The boat crews, camped for the night near Petersburg, Alaska, enjoyed "no small portion of mirth . . . in consequence of . . . having sailed from old England on the *first of April*, for the purpose of discovering a northwest passage, following up the discoveries of de Fuca, de Fonte, and a numerous train of hypothetical navigators."

For three years, Vancouver had worked to put an end to speculation about a passage leading east through North America. That task now accomplished, he ordered an extra measure of grog all round, then gave the crews a holiday. The following day, they sailed for Nootka. At Nootka, the ships were prepared for the long voyage home. On October 16, the *Discovery* and the *Chatham* left the northwest coast for the last time.

Though Vancouver had been instructed not to put ashore in Spanish territory, he disobeyed his orders, and anchored at Valparaiso, in South America, to replace a mast and to obtain fresh water and wood. In poor health now, he stayed ashore with the Spanish governor. Though he had instructions to survey the coast to the south, he did not do so: the ships, at sea more than three years, were in bad shape, their sails worn and rotted, their masts oft-repaired. Neither they, nor their crews, nor Vancouver himself, could face more months of hard duty. Instead, he continued on around the Horn, and sailed into the Atlantic.

His quarrels with his officers continued. Menzies had a servant whose duty it was to care for the precious plants Menzies had collected in three years' travel and kept alive under a glass frame on the quarterdeck. An officer ordered the servant onto regular watch; the frames were left uncovered and the plants destroyed. Beside himself over the destruction of the samples he had preserved so long for the gardens of the Royal Society, Menzies raged at Vancouver. Vancouver had Menzies arrested and charged him with insolence and contempt. He later withdrew the charges when Menzies apologized, but relations between the two were not repairable.

By October, Vancouver was back in England. The *Discovery* and *Chatham* had sailed more than a hundred thousand kilometres; their boats had covered another sixteen thousand, most of it under oars. Vancouver had filled in the map of America's northwest coast in intricate and

skillful detail.

Yet he received little acclaim, and less money. The admiralty took four years to pay the wages they owed Vancouver; the small amount they allowed barely covered his debts. Vancouver's treatment of his midshipmen came home to haunt him: the Baron Camelford, by all accounts at least as irascible as Vancouver and possibly deranged, chased his former captain down a London street and challenged him to a duel. The London papers cruelly caricatured Vancouver over the undignified incident.

In ever worsening health, Vancouver retired to the countryside to finish his diaries and maps and prepare them for publication. On May 12, 1798, just after he had read the proofs for a book on his voyages, a book he hoped would bring him fame and fortune, he died, possibly of a chronic thyroid condition. He was just forty years of age.

Alexander Mackenzie: Pioneer by Land

On the third of June, 1793, Captain George Vancouver had breakfast by the side of a long arm of the sea that cut between ranks of mountains towards the mouth of the Bella Coola River. Seven weeks later, Alexander Mackenzie, the first European to cross North America by land, painted a message on a rock beside this same channel, to mark his arrival at the sea.

That Vancouver and Mackenzie came so close to meeting was, in one way, sheer coincidence. One sailed from England, for king and country. One walked and canoed across the continent, for the interests of the commercial company that sent him. Yet

In 1793 the grizzly bear was still common east of the Rockies. Mackenzie and his men were well aware of the danger of these animals when they were sighted along the Peace River.

both men were driven by that desire so strong in the last decades of the eighteenth century, to explore, to claim and to exploit a region almost unknown to white men.

Alexander Mackenzie was born in 1764, near Stornoway, on the bleak and stony island of Lewis in the Outer Hebrides. When

Mackenzie noted the special character of the Rainbow Mountains, known to local natives as the Bleeding Mountains. Long red, yellow, magenta and black streaks sweep down from loose gravelly ridges. Large snow patches survive late in the year at these high elevations, as was the case when Mackenzie travelled through in July of 1793.

"In the counting house of Mr. Gregory I had been five years; and at this period had left him ... to seek my fortune at Detroit. He admitted a partner in this business, on condition that I would proceed to the Indian country in the following spring, 1785. ... I readily assented to [the condition] and immediately proceeded to the Grande Portage." — From Mackenzie's "General History of the Fur Trade."

he was ten, his mother died, and his father, Kenneth, took him to New York, leaving behind two daughters. New York was not hospitable for long: the American Revolutionary War broke out soon after the Mackenzies arrived, and Kenneth, a staunch Royalist, joined a Loyalist regiment. Alexander was sent to safety, first north to the Mohawk Valley, then to Montreal. Kenneth Mackenzie died not long after, apparently of scurvy.

The fifteen-year-old orphan found a job as a clerk for the counting-house of Finlay, Gregory and Company. Little wonder that he felt at home there: transplanted Scots — Finlays, Gregorys, Camerons, Frasers, Grants, McDonalds, McDougalls, McGillivrays — dominated the companies trading for furs out of Montreal into the west country in the 1770s. James Finlay was one of the first "pedlars from Montreal" to challenge the fur-trading monopoly held by the Hudson's Bay Company over the vast, fur-rich regions west and south of Hudson Bay. No stay-at-home like the traders who manned the posts on the bay, Finlay made the three-thousand-kilometre trek inland to the Saskatchewan River, where he built a trading post and began trade with the natives of the prairies.

Mackenzie put in a five-year stint in the counting house, working hard and waiting for the time when he would be asked to go west. In 1784, he made his first trading trip, to the Detroit area. But the end of the American revolutionary war meant that Canadian companies trading out of Montreal must build new posts north of the newly independent United States. Mackenzie was offered a partnership in the company, if he would work in the *pays*

d'en haut — the country west of the Great Lakes.

Mackenzie accepted happily. The west country drew him, and he welcomed the chance to explore and trade there. He was dispatched to the English River department, to the trading post of Ile à la Crosse, on the upper Churchill River. Two years after he arrived, his company merged with the North West Company, the banner now jointly raised by previously warring smaller companies that had joined together to reduce competition, pool resources, and outface — and out-trade — the Hudson's Bay Company. The company was composed of Montreal partners who received the furs from the hinterland and sold them in Europe, and wintering partners, who travelled and traded in the northwest.

Mackenzie was dispatched to the Athabasca country as second-in-command to Nor'Wester Peter Pond. Pond was a renegade in the fur trade, a man of violent temper, suspected of killing two of his rivals. But, more than any man, he knew the country. Mackenzie spent the winter of 1787-88 with Pond in Athabasca, learning from the master. When Pond left the country that spring, he reported he had left Mackenzie with a mission: to find and follow a great river Pond was convinced flowed from the Athabasca country to Cook's Inlet, on the south coast of Alaska. Mackenzie had been told, said Pond, to make his way from the river's mouth to Unalaska, to Kamchatka on the Siberian coast, and thence home by whatever means he could.

Mackenzie was eager to comply with Pond's wishes. Twenty-five years old in 1789, he was a four-year veteran of the

Athabasca country, tall, husky, strong, determined. He was, he said himself long after, "endowed by Nature with an inquisitive and enterprising spirit; possessing also a constitution and frame of body equal to the most arduous undertakings . . . familiar with toilsome exertions." Ambitious and energetic, he made preparations for a trip that would prove or deny Pond's theories. Quite possibly, he told the company nothing of his plans; no proof remains, one way or the other, but Mackenzie was not a man to worry about permission.

The young fur trader set off from Fort Chipewyan on Lake Athabasca, where he had moved his headquarters, on June 3, 1789, along with four French-Canadian voyageurs to paddle the canoe, a young German and a group of Chipewyan natives who would act as guides and hunters.

For forty days, they paddled down the rivers that led northwards, seeking directions and information from groups of natives they met along their route. Twenty-five hundred kilometres downstream, Mackenzie realized by the taste of the river water that he had reached salt water. He was greatly disappointed: though his scientific training was limited, all his observations suggested the group was too far north and too far east for this to be the Pacific Ocean. He named the river that had borne him to the sea the River of Disappointment; now it is known as the Mackenzie River.

Mackenzie and his companions spent three days near the edge of the Arctic Ocean, then set themselves to the more arduous task of paddling back upstream to Lake Athabasca. In fifty-nine days, they arrived back at Fort Chipewyan.

He was indeed disappointed by the results of his travels, but he was not convinced that the idea behind the trip was wrong: another overland route must exist that would take him to the Pacific. Through the course of the next two years, spent trading and travelling through the Athabasca district, he considered where his next explorations would take him. In the autumn of 1791, he went down to Montreal, then crossed the Atlantic to London. He knew his trade — the fur trade — and he knew how to travel over and live off the land. But he knew little about the theory of geography and map-making. "[I was] not only without the necessary books and instruments," he wrote many years later, "but also felt . . . deficient in the sciences of astronomy and navigation; I did not hesitate, therefore, to undertake a winter's voyage to this country [England], in order to procure the one and acquire the other. These objects being accomplished, I returned, to determine the practicability of a commercial communication through the continent of North American, between the Atlantic and Pacific Oceans."

Mackenzie decided that he would venture west once more in the spring of 1793. So that he could begin his journey from as far west as possible, he sent two men up the Peace River, to square timbers for a house and a palisade to surround it. In October of 1792, he set out from Lake Athabasca for the Peace River. Sailing and paddling their canoes, he and his voyageurs raced against the ice that was beginning to form each night on the river, to join the men dispatched the previous spring at Fort Fork, near present-day Peace River, Alberta. Mackenzie pitched his tent, discussed his plans with the local natives who came to

"I happened to wake about 4 this Morning. I was surprized to observe the water had come under our Baggage as the wind had not changed nor blew harder than when we went to Bed. I wakened my Men to move the Baggage &c. We were all of the Opinion that it was the Tide." — Mackenzie reaches Arctic tidewater, July 15, 1789.

"*My winter interpreter . . . shed tears on the reflection of those dangers which we might encounter in our expedition, while my own people offered up their prayers that we might return in safety from it.*" — *May 9, 1792*

Mackenzie and his men, working against an increasing current on the Peace River between present-day Fort St. John and Hudson's Hope, had to travel on foot along steep slippery banks, always in danger of falling into the frigid waters below.

meet him, and set his men to work building a fort. That accomplished, he spent the winter contemplating his future and trading for what few furs the Cree brought in.

The long, lonely winter, and the contrast to the winter he had spent in England, ate into his single-mindedness and his determination to venture west. "I was never so undecided in my intentions as this year," he wrote to his cousin Roderic, also a fur trader, "regarding my going to the Portage or remaining in land, I weighed everything in my mind and over again." But his desire to be the man who found a passage overland outweighed his doubts. "I would not have remained [in the west], had I any intention of continuing in this country beyond the insuing winter," he told Roderic. "Should I be successful, I shall retire to greater advantage. Should I not be successful I cannot be worse off than I am at present. I begin to think it is the highth of folly in a man to reside in a country of this kind, deprived of every comfort that can render life agreeable, especially when he has a competency to enjoy life in civilised society which will or ought to be the case with me." This voyage, triumph or failure, would be Mackenzie's last venture in the northwest.

Mackenzie was convinced, partly because Pond had been equally convinced, that the Pacific was not far distant. On May 9, Mackenzie and his ten men wrestled their canoe, almost eight metres long, loaded with a tonne and a half of provisions, presents, arms, ammunition, and baggage, into the waters of the Peace River, and set out between riverbanks dotted with pink and purple wildflowers.

In two days of paddling, they reached the foothills of the Rockies. In his diary, Mackenzie recorded groves of poplars, vast herds of elk and buffalo, trees with newly opened blossoms, the rays of a rising or setting sun shining through the young velvet on the tree branches: "a succession of the most beautiful scenery I had ever seen." The strong current obliged them to set their poles into the river bottom and

*The Peace River near
Hudson's Hope presents a
tranquil picture now, as in
Mackenzie's day. The
tranquillity ended
abruptly; the violence of
the Peace River Canyon lay
ahead.*

Huge herds of Rocky Mountain elk once inhabited the eastern slopes of the Rockies. Mackenzie was to discover, however, that the country west of the mountain range supported far fewer large mammals than the great plains, and his party was forced to rely for food on hard rations and the generosity of native people they met.

haul the canoe upstream. Slowly, they moved into the mountains. Mackenzie was looking for an old man, a Rocky Mountain native he had met the winter before, who had already told him much about the country ahead. But the man was not to be found, and Mackenzie went on, relying on the information the native had provided and on local guides, noting that "without them I should not have attempted to proceed."

The pattern of the trip was soon established. They were on the river at 4 A.M., paddling, poling, sailing, as current and wind permitted. At seven at night, they

pulled in to shore, to make camp, have supper and sleep. They crossed what is now the Alberta-British Columbia border on May 14, and caught their first sight of the Rockies themselves on May 17. On May 19, they reached the lower end of the Peace River Canyon. The natives who lived here told Mackenzie the river could not be ascended by canoe: rapids and cascades blocked the way west, and Mackenzie and his men would have to unload their canoe and portage along the trail the natives used, a day's march to calmer water.

This was not what Mackenzie wanted to hear. Long portages would be a serious inconvenience on any commercial route to the west. Headstrong and convinced he was right, Mackenzie refused the advice. He had been, he wrote later, with understatement, "greatly displeased that so much time had been lost," and ordered his men to cross the river and tow the canoe along the opposite shore. Waves and current drove the canoe violently against the stony shore and damaged the boat badly. Now the folly of Mackenzie's course became apparent. He could turn back, or he could try an extremely dangerous traverse of the river, back to the original side, where the men could try again to tow the canoe along the shore. The traverse was made, and the men hauled the canoe along at the end of a hundred-metre line, unloading it and carrying gear across points of land where this was unavoidable. Rocks rolled down on the men from overhanging cliffs; though Mackenzie was in no personal danger, since he and the men not needed to move the canoe took a safer route farther from the river's bank, he confessed he was worried, noting in his journal, "nor was my solicitude diminished by my [being] necessarily removed at times from the sight of them."

By five in the afternoon, the canoe was in water so violent that all their strength just barely served to prevent its being dashed to pieces. They unloaded the canoe again and lined it up the canyon "through one continued rapid," guided by the few brave men who remained aboard to paddle and steer. A wave broke on the bow; the line snapped. Nothing, it seemed, could save the canoe from disaster and the men in it from death. Their luck held. A second wave drove the canoe toward the shore. Prudent at last, Mackenzie halted, deciding

not to challenge the "white sheet of foaming water" that lay ahead.

Though, incredibly, the canoe was unharmed, the men were disenchanted. "Indeed," wrote Mackenzie, "it began to be muttered on all sides that there was no alternative but to return." But Mackenzie was not a man to be deterred by the mutterings of his men. Prudence might be in his vocabulary; consensus was not. He set the dissenters to work, climbing the hill that closed in on the river, and making camp. Until last light, he followed the river's bank himself, but he saw no end ahead to the rapids. He decided that the group must climb out of the canyon, and portage their way to smoother water.

The next morning, rain teemed down. Deeming discretion — and a longer night's sleep — the better part of leadership, he allowed his followers to sleep in until 8 A.M. "As the men have been very fatigued and disheartened," he wrote, "I suffered them to continue their rest." He then sent out exploring parties, who confirmed that the only possible course was to seek the Indian portage route. Over a dinner of wild rice sweetened with sugar and a tot of rum, all decided that the next day their difficulties would be surmounted.

On May 22, starting at daybreak, the men cut a road up the mountain behind them, felling trees and using them as railings up either side of the path, and hauling themselves and their gear hand over hand upwards along the railings. They brought the canoe up by fastening the line to successive stumps and warping it to the summit.

It took two days to cover the eleven kilometres from the foot to the head of the

*The Peace is the only
B.C. river to cut through
the Rocky Mountains
from west to east. When
Mackenzie first glimpsed
the summits of the
Rockies, he was following
the advice of an old
native man. Now he had
to find a way through
them, travel a thousand
kilometres through
unknown territory to the
sea — and be back
before winter.*

rapids. When they returned to the river, they looked back with horror at the seething water they had avoided: "It was really awful to behold with what infinite force the water drives against the rocks on one side, and with what impetuous strength it is impelled to the other; it then falls back into a more strait but rugged passage, over which it is tossed in high, foaming, half-formed billows."

The next day, they cut new poles for the canoe, repaired the damages wrought by the river and the portage, and repacked their goods into the canoe. From here on, the river was less hair-raising — so much changed that Mackenzie reported, without embarrassment, that he could not give the exact courses of the river for a week or so, since he lost the book in which he recorded them, probably when tree branches brushed it away during one of the naps he could now take as the voyageurs paddled upstream.

On May 31, they came to the place where the Parsnip and the Finlay rivers join together to form the Peace. Both Mackenzie and his men thought the river that tended northwest looked more promising, but Mackenzie remembered the words of the old man who had travelled here many years before. Avoid the north fork, he warned, for that river soon divides into many branches that lose themselves in the mountains. The south fork, according to the old man, would take them to a carrying place. Across the carrying place lay a large river that led to the sea. The men argued: the current on the south fork was too strong, the journey would be too long. But they obeyed.

They paddled and poled upriver, hard

These eroded islets topped with greenery attest to the force of the river in flood. Mackenzie noted them as he began encountering the difficult waters approaching the Peace Canyon, about a kilometre downstream from today's Hudson's Hope.

"*At two in the afternoon the Rocky Mountains appeared in sight, with their summits covered with snow, bearing Sout-west by South: they formed a very agreeable object to every person in the canoe, as we attained the view of them much sooner than we expected.*" — *May 17, 1793*

tedious work, plagued first by freezing cold, then by oppressive heat, into country where gnats and mosquitoes tormented them from sunrise to sundown. Though he revealed no anxiety to his men, Mackenzie now began to doubt his course. He left the canoe while he and several others climbed a mountain, then almost panicked when he could not find the canoe again. "My

*"*And here I could not but reflect, with infinite anxiety, on the hazard of my enterprize: one false step of those who were attached to the line, or the breaking of the line itself, would have at once consigned the canoe, and every thing it contained, to instant destruction."* — May 19, 1793*

mind was in a state of extreme agitation; and the imprudence of my conduct in leaving the people, in such a situation of danger and toilsome exertion, added a very painful mortification to the severe apprehension I had already suffered; it was an act of indiscretion which might have put an end to the voyage that I had so much at heart."

Eventually, Mackenzie found his canoe. Some distance on, he tried to discover from Sekani Indians whom he met the location of the carrying place that would take him to the river that led to the sea. They expressed ignorance; without their help, Mackenzie knew, he could not continue. What should he do? "Various projects presented themselves to my mind, which were no sooner formed than they were discovered to be impracticable, and were consequently abandoned." He could go overland, on an eleven-day march the Sekani said led to the land of the coastal people — but he and his men could not carry enough food to sustain them on the journey, or enough presents to trade for food or help, or ammunition to hunt. He did not have enough time to stay with the Sekani until they chose to go to the sea. To continue up the river, ignorant, could not work. To return was unthinkable. Was the interpreter telling the truth, or was he hiding it, more interested in returning home than continuing on? Mackenzie could

The Peace River today, tamed with dams, is no longer the raging obstacle of Mackenzie's time. But the same sandstone ledges still cause enough whitewater, especially during runoff, to be a threat to modern-day canoeists with better equipment than Mackenzie.

not tell. But he decided to wait, in the hope that the Sekani would help.

They did. One of the Sekani drew a map for Mackenzie, using coal on a strip of bark, and another agreed to act as a guide, to take them to the great river that led to the sea. On June 10, they embarked once more. A day later, they left the main branch of the Parsnip River, and turned into a smaller stream, narrow and meandering. Another day's journey brought them to the source of this stream; they disembarked to follow a path beaten over a low ridge. Eight hundred and seventeen paces later, they reached a tributary of the Fraser River; they had crossed the divide between the waters that flow to the Arctic Ocean and those that flow to the Pacific.

The confluence of the Fraser River and the West Road River, now called the Blackwater, can be glimpsed through the thick forest of the Fraser Plateau near Quesnel. Near here Mackenzie abandoned the Fraser (which he thought was the Columbia) and opted for an overland route to the sea.

"*At five in the afternoon we arrived on the banks of another lake, when it again threatened rain ... we accordingly fixed our shed, the rain continuing with great violence through the remainder of the day: it was, therefore, determined that we stop here for the night.*" — July 5, 1793

Soaking wet from a day slogging through the bush from the Fraser River westward, and with another storm on the horizon, the party made camp early near Cleswuncut Lake, northwest of Quesnel. The site is now part of a historic hiking trail roughly following Mackenzie's original route.

The tributary Mackenzie named the Bad River. Scummy, smelly, icy cold, and rapid, the creek was obstructed by gravel banks and fallen trees. The Sekani guide, considering his job done and hating the river, wanted to return home. On their second day on the Bad River — now known as James Creek — Mackenzie decided the canoe should be unloaded and taken downstream by a few of his men. "Those in the boat," he noted, wanted him to go with them, "[so] that, if they perished, I should perish with them." Mackenzie's vaunted leadership was meeting with doubt. "I did not then imagine in how short a period their apprehension would be justified."

Almost immediately, the current swung the canoe sideways and drove it downriver into a sandbar. The men jumped out, but the water deepened, and they were forced to jump back in to save their lives. The water pushed the canoe against a rock; the collision shattered the stern. Then the current washed the canoe across the creek, and a second rock shattered the bow. The foreman seized the branches of an overhanging tree to stop the canoe — but the branches whipped him out of the boat. The canoe carried Mackenzie and the oarsmen into a cascade that broke holes in the bottom — fortunately, for the boat now became "flat upon the water" and slightly more manageable. Everyone jumped out, and the steersman called upon all to save themselves.

Mackenzie countermanded: hang on, he yelled. They did. The current bore the battered hulk into a small eddy, where it caught on the bottom and halted. The natives wept, the boatmen wailed, and Mackenzie could scarcely get to his feet,
so numb were his legs from cold water and nerves.

In the chaos, all their ammunition was lost overboard; only their powder remained. In camp that night, the crewmen talked themselves into a stupor, and Mackenzie ordered rum all round. He then rallied his crew with a speech that must have called upon all the resources of his young brain. Be thankful we escaped, he exhorted; we got into this trouble only because we didn't know where we were going. Now we have passed the worst, we will be safer. I never told you this would be easy, he said. But if we succeed, we shall have honours heaped on us; if we go home failures, we shall all be disgraced. Surely, he said, you men of the north have more courage, more resolution, than most men. We will build a new canoe; we will go on. We will reach the Pacific.

Perhaps against reason, the men were convinced. They pledged to follow Mackenzie wherever he chose to go. He sent men downriver to trace the course of the creek. They reported that the creek itself did not improve, but that they had caught sight of a large river in the distance. The men repaired the canoe just enough that they could proceed, then continued downriver, walking and paddling.

They reached the Fraser River on June 18. Their guide had by now decamped, convinced, one assumes, that there was no point in facing continual danger on a project that must have had little significance for the Sekani. Now, from three each morning till seven each night, they swept down the Fraser, portaging past the Fort George canyon. Their canoe, which once could be portaged with ease, was now so

After several days of combatting mosquitoes, swamps and hunger, Mackenzie ascended a valley into the alpine region of the Rainbow Ranges.

heavy with gum and bark that two men could not carry it a hundred metres without resting, and ''cracked and broke on the shoulders of the men who bore her.'' By June 20, Mackenzie decided the canoe had become so ''crazy'' that a new one must be built.

The next few days were passed in getting bark for a new canoe, bargaining with the Carrier natives they met for food and information, and moving on downriver in the old canoe, by now so leaky that it half-filled with water in every rapid. In one Carrier village, an old man drew them a sketch map on a piece of bark, describing the course of the river ahead. It was, he said, blocked by many falls and rapids, with portages of great length over hills and mountains. Three other tribes lived, in succession, along its banks. The sea was far distant, at the river's mouth. But there was, the Carrier said, another route to the sea. Mackenzie must return upstream and strike out overland along a well-travelled native path that led along lakes and rivers, six days' travel, to the ocean's edge, where lived a people who traded iron, copper, brass and beads in return for the furs and dressed leather the Carriers offered.

Mackenzie was convinced. The more he heard about the river they were on, the more convinced he was that it was not the river he wanted. The distance to the ocean was too great, for he had no more than thirty days' food remaining, no bullets, and not much time if he were to return to Fort Fork before the winter. He decided to return back up the river, to take the trade route to the coast.

Mackenzie didn't let his change of heart dent his air of omniscience. When a Carrier

Scores of tiny, pristine lakes dot the landscape around Mackenzie Pass, which remains today much as it was two hundred years ago.

asked why, if the white man knew everything in the world, they sought so assiduously for information about this country, Mackenzie soon found a reply. He did, he answered, certainly know where the sea was and where he himself was, but he did not know exactly what lay between the two. He was happy to ask the Carriers about this, for they had so often made the trip. "Thus," wrote Mackenzie in his journal for June 23, perhaps with wishful thinking, "I fortunately preserved the impression in their minds, of the superiority of white people over themselves."

Mackenzie announced the new plans to his men, and told them he would go on alone if he had to. They demurred: they would follow him wherever he chose to go. A day later, after their Carrier guide had led them, very rapidly, through some "very bad ways," they were less sure. Exhausted, cold, wet, hungry, and terrified that the Carrier were about to attack, they panicked. The trip, they said, could not be made. But Mackenzie was, as usual, impervious. "Let us reimbark and be gone," the men shouted. "This, however," Mackenzie recollected in tranquillity years later, "was not my design. . . . [In] a more peremptory tone than I usually employed, they were ordered to unload the canoe and take her out of the water." The men were bad-tempered, and, by this time, so was he. But he had no intention of turning back; to turn back would be to admit failure, and that thought alone renewed his resolve.

"*Our way was now nearly level, without the least snow, and not a tree to be seen in any part of it.*" — *July 17, 1793*

As each new revolt began, he used every technique he could devise to persuade the men to go on. When he thought it wise, he spoke to them as a group. Sometimes, he spoke to them one by one; to one "more disposed to eat than to be active," he averred that whatever the men decided to do, Mackenzie would never turn back, "in spite of every difficulty that might oppose,

Alexander Mackenzie: Pioneer by Land   61

or danger that should threaten.'' Perhaps more afraid of returning without him than of proceeding with him, the men always went on.

By now, they had completed a new canoe, and sealed it with gum from the old. On July 3, they turned west along the West Road (Blackwater) River looking for the guides Mackenzie thought he had hired but who had not turned up; to go on without them would be impossible. In their own time, the guides appeared, and the group prepared for their overland journey. The next morning, they cached their canoe and whatever provisions they could not carry with them, and started west on foot. Each of the Canadian voyageurs carried a forty-kilogram pack, plus a gun and ammunition. Mackenzie and his second-in-command carried about thirty kilos each. Mackenzie noted that the Carrier who accompanied them were unhappy when asked to carry twenty kilos each, since their custom was to hunt for food, not to carry it with them.

Their days on the trail westward fell into a routine: out early in the morning on a road that Mackenzie describes as well-traced, talking to the natives they met along the way, persuading new guides to accompany them for a few days, trading for food. In some ways, they were the first — now typical — Chilcotin tourists, always in more of a hurry than the people who lived in the Chilcotin, worrying about what they would eat, trying to get their guides to hurry, trying to change the habits of guides who knew what they were doing and were determined to do it at their own pace. Mackenzie and his men were handed on from group to group along the trade trail;

some of their new acquaintances told them stories about the whites who had visited the coast in huge canoes with sails. A week into their trek, they caught first sight of the coast mountains. Though rain, mud and insects depressed them, the idea that the sea was not far distant restored their spirits.

Mackenzie was in a hurry; the Chilcotin he travelled with were not. At length, his guides decided they would go off in a different direction, but that another group who would soon arrive would guide Mackenzie across the mountains. Mackenzie liked his guides; he vowed he would go where they went, anticipating that they would take him across the mountains after all. But they had had enough. They boiled up a kettle of fish roe for the white men, to supplement their remaining pemmican, and departed — but not before new guides arrived. The new guides took the party west again, through swamp and burned-off forest, into the beautiful valley that now bears Mackenzie's name.

Now they climbed through hardened snow, through hail and snow and rain, through buffeting wind. It was, wrote Mackenzie, ''weather as distressing as any

"*Before us appeared a stupendous mountain, whose snow-clad summit was lost in clouds; between it and our immediate course flowed the river to which we were going.*" — *July 17, 1793*

lect enough wood, they built a fire, and cooked and wolfed down the meat.

Now the mountains seemed to draw apart, revealing open country and a series of precipices. Below them lay the Bella Coola River. They had crossed the height of land between the waters that flowed to the Fraser and then to the Pacific, and those that flowed directly to the ocean. In celebration, Mackenzie shaved and changed his linen; his men followed suit. Like every subsequent traveller, they were struck by the transition to the coastal forest, with the largest and loftiest cedar trees they had ever seen. "We were now sensible of an entire change in climate," Mackenzie wrote, "and the berries were quite ripe." And, like any other tourist who makes it down the series of precipices that make up the Big Hill into the Bella Coola Valley, they congratulated themselves and ate a hearty dinner — roast salmon, salmon roe, gooseberries and sorrel, prepared by the Bella Coola natives — and went to bed. "I never," wrote Mackenzie, "enjoyed a more sound and refreshing rest, though I had a board for my bed and a billet for my pillow."

Breakfast was berries and roasted salmon. Mackenzie was greatly impressed by the river, and by the multitude of salmon that fought their way up it to spawn. The men offended religious beliefs almost at once: one of them threw a deer bone into the river. A Bella Coolan dove in and retrieved it, threw it into the fire, and washed his hands: no smell or touch of animal flesh must be allowed to pollute their river and scare away the salmon. Mackenzie realized that the Bella Coolans feared he would take venison aboard any canoe he borrowed, and thus contaminate

The Bella Coola Valley is a beautiful area with mist-shrouded mountain peaks, where eagles watch totemlike from the giant cottonwood snags along the river. Here Mackenzie received help from native people, who supplied provisions and transportation for the last leg of his journey to the sea.

I had ever experienced." The hunters shot a small deer, all they could bag though they fired twelve shots through the swirling hail and snow; Mackenzie suggested they leave half the venison cached, but the men insisted on carrying it, though they were exhausted. Ahead of them, the sky cleared enough for them to catch sight of a "stupendous mountain" now called Stupendous Mountain. As soon as they could col-

Tidewater at Bella Coola marked the site of Mackenzie's triumph and failure. Although he had reached the sea, he had not achieved his goal of finding the Columbia River and thus a viable trade route to the Pacific.

"*At about eight we got out of the river, which discharges itself by various channels into an arm of the sea.*" — *July 20, 1793*

the river. He quickly promised not to do so and was granted a canoe. He also asked for salmon to take on his journey, but by now the chief's hospitality was wearing thin. Make haste, be on your way, suggested the chief; the current will take you to the next village.

And so they left, continuing on downriver, their canoes paddled by Bella Coolans Mackenzie judged the best canoe men in

the world, better even than his own voyageurs. Late in the evening of July 19, he saw what he had sought for so many years. From a village near the mouth of the Bella Coola River, Mackenzie "could perceive the termination of the river, and its discharge into a narrow arm of the sea."

“*The face of the hills, where they are not enlivened with verdure, appears at a distance as if fire had passed over them.*” — *July 17, 1793*

canoe, and continued out into the ocean. The men saw the tide ebb and swell, watched sea otters and porpoises leap and dive, helped eat a porcupine a young chief killed. Though his voyageurs were horrified at the thought, Mackenzie and his lieutenant McKay boiled and ate shellfish McKay scraped off rocks.

On the evening of July 21, they landed and camped on a rock at the channel's edge. The next day, he wrote his famous message: "I now mixed up some vermilion in melted grease, and inscribed, in large characters, on the South-East face of the rock on which we had slept last night, this brief memorial — 'Alexander Mackenzie, from Canada, by land, the twenty-second of July, one thousand, seven hundred and ninety-three.' " His aim achieved, Mackenzie could now turn back.

But he had passed from the territory of the Bella Coola Indians, who had been hospitable, to that of the Bella Bellans, who were less so. Just weeks before, reported Bella Bella men in three canoes, they had met Vancouver. Some of them said Vancouver had treated them badly. The Bella Bellans pursued Mackenzie and frightened his men, who raced for the river and fought the rapids back upstream. Once more, the men turned mutinous. Mackenzie had to argue, expostulate and convince them yet again that they should follow him.

They left behind the friendly village where the Bella Coolans had treated them so well, and took once more to the trail, each man carrying ten kilos of fish in addition to his regular pack. Though climbing back to the mountain pass exhausted them, they could not but be enchanted by the scenery before them: the depth of the

The Rainbow Mountains, now part of Tweedsmuir Provincial Park, along the Alexander Mackenzie Heritage Trail. A mountain pass and the valley leading to it bear Mackenzie's name in honour of his great physical achievement.

Some might think his task complete — but Mackenzie wanted to go on. The Bella Coolans could not imagine what else he might want, since he had now seen the sea he had been so anxious to reach. Mackenzie persuaded them to lend him another

The Rainbow Range impressed Mackenzie on his westbound trip, but by the time he returned he was blasé, writing only that "there was little or no change in the appearance of the mountains since we passed them."

precipices below, the height of the mountains above, the "rude and wild magnificence" of the country around.

They crossed the pass, and began the descent. Eager to be home and retracing familiar ground, Mackenzie now wrote less and less in his journal. Ten days after they left Friendly Village, they arrived back at their cache of canoe and supplies. Reclaiming their supplies and reloading their canoe, they paddled back to the Bad River, which they had hated, descending, and hated, ascending. Mackenzie's ankles swelled so badly in the ascent that he could not walk, and he had to be carried across the 817 paces between the watersheds of the Fraser and the Peace.

By 7:30 of the morning of Saturday, August 17, they were back on the Parsnip River, gliding down with the current they had fought on the way up. In one day, they returned the distance it had taken them seven days to advance. In three days, they were back at the Peace River Canyon, on very short rations and anxious to portage to the lower end.

Farther down the river, one of their hunters shot an elk. "To give some notion of our appetites, I shall state the elk, or at least the carcase of it, which we brought away, to have weighed two hundred and fifty pounds; and as we had taken a very hearty meal at one o'clock, it might naturally be supposed that we should not be very voracious at supper; nevertheless, a kettle full of the elk flesh was boiled and eaten, and that vessel replenished and put on the fire. All that remained with the bones, &c. was placed, after the Indian fashion round the fire to roast, and at ten the next morning the whole was consumed by ten persons and a large dog."

On August 24, in sunshine and summer heat, they landed at Fort Fork, three months after they had left. Mackenzie's second epic expedition was over. He had pushed himself and his men nineteen hundred kilometres in seventy-four days, averaging thirty-two kilometres a day, fifty-seven on the days when they were on the water. Though he could not have made the trip without the help of the native people he had met, his accomplishment and that of his men was still well beyond that of any other white fur trader.

He remained that winter at Fort Chipewyan, spending what was undoubtedly the worst winter of his life. After the intensity and action of his summer, the inactivity of a winter at an isolated trading post was scarcely to be borne. He decided he was through with the northwest. "I think it unpardonable," he wrote to cousin Roderic in January, "in any man to remain in this country who can afford to leave it. What a pretty Situation I am in this winter. Starving and alone, without the power of doing myself or any body any Service. The Boy at Lac La Loche, or even my own Servant, is equal to the performance of my winter employment."

Mackenzie could not even complete the task of setting the journal of his trip in order. "Last fall I was to begin copying it, but the greatest part of my time was taken up in vain Speculations. I got into such a habit of thinking that I was often lost in thoughts nor could I ever write to the purpose. What I was thinking of, would often occur to me instead of that which I ought to do. I never passed so much of my time insignificantly, nor so uneasy." If he closed his eyes to sleep, he was pursued by dreams and visions of the dead.

It was not a life for a man of action. In the spring of 1794, just turned thirty years of age, Alexander Mackenzie left the north country forever. He went out with the fur brigades from Athabasca to Grand Portage, for the annual meeting between the wintering partners and the Montreal partners in the Northwest Company.

The meeting was acrimonious. The wintering partners clamoured for more influence in the company; they thought they had been slighted in the distribution of shares. Mackenzie agreed. A vigorous advocate of those who worked in the northwest and endured its weather and its difficulties, he carried the argument of the wintering partners down to Montreal, where he convinced the Montreal partners to give more to the men he represented. The following year, now an agent from Montreal, he argued again for his colleagues, and again won more for them.

In Montreal, Mackenzie shared bachelor quarters with William McGillivray, a fellow Nor'Wester, and did the drinking and carousing that he had so missed in the north country. But his entertainment did not blind him to his purpose. His experiences and travel had convinced him that the North West Company must develop trade routes across the country to the Pacific, and to the Orient. The company must, he demanded, persuade the Hudson's Bay Company to let them ship supplies from the bay to Athabasca. Furs gathered in the west should travel west, to the Pacific and thence to China.

His demands were not well received. Any diversion of furs and supplies from Montreal would lessen both the influence and the profits of the Montreal partners. It would make Montreal just another depot in the trade, instead of the company headquarters. Mackenzie's ideas were ignored or shunted aside.

In 1799, Mackenzie's agreement with the North West Company expired. Frustrated by the fact that he could make no headway, he announced he would withdraw from it. Though the wintering partners urged him to stay, it is probable that the Montreal partners were glad to see him go.

Over the next few years, Mackenzie tried to devise a new future in the fur trade. He tried to return to the Nor'Westers, then joined forces with a new and opposing company. But even though his old antagonist and nemesis Simon McTavish died in 1804, there was no longer a place in the fur trade for Alexander Mackenzie. He became a celebrity when the edited version of his journals was published; he was knighted in 1802, and was elected a member of the Legislative Assembly of Lower Canada. But he had little interest in politics, and his long-time fascination with the fur trade had faded. By 1805, he had moved to London for good.

In 1810, he made his last visit to Canada. Two years later, now forty-eight, he married a young — perhaps as young as thirteen — Scottish girl; the couple had three children.

Ill health, diagnosed by later biographers as the chronic kidney inflammation known as Bright's disease, plagued him. "The exercise of walking," he wrote to Roderic, "particularly if uphill, brings on a

headache, stupor or dead pain which at once pervades the whole frame, attended with a listlessness and apathy I cannot well describe,'' a complaint that the man who crossed a continent might well find unbearable. In 1820, aged fifty-six, on the way back from a trip to the doctor, he died.

Simon Fraser: Untutored, Undeterred

The beaver, almost extinct east of the Rockies because of overtrapping, was thriving in British Columbia. The sight must have buoyed Fraser's spirits as he continued his search for better routes to get the furs to market.

Alexander Mackenzie lost his battle to expand the fur trade westward, but time and change achieved what he could not. In 1808, three years after Mackenzie left Canada for London, a new North West Company exploring expedition set the bows of four canoes into the current of the Great River that Mackenzie had abandoned in his quest for the Pacific.

In the fifteen years since Mackenzie's trip, much had changed. Fur trader James Finlay had ventured from the head of the Peace River canyon north and south along the Parsnip and the Finlay. Nor'Westers David Thompson and Duncan McGillivray had taken their first tentative steps from the North Saskatchewan River into the passes through the Rocky Mountains. Most important, the feuds that had sapped the energy and the resources of the North West Company had ended with the death of Simon McTavish, and the departure of Mackenzie himself. The warring companies

For Fraser, only the most inclement of weather would stop progress. He always rose early to check weather conditions; very occasionally would they result in a delay in getting on the river.

joined together; the new North West Company, strengthened and single-minded, could turn its undivided attention to the fur trade west of the Rocky Mountains.

No definite evidence exists to show when the company decided to establish trading posts west of the Rockies. The decision was probably taken, however, at the summer meeting of the wintering and Montreal partners at Fort William in 1805, and Simon Fraser was chosen to lead an expedition across the Rockies.

Like Mackenzie and most of the other North West Company partners, Fraser was a Scotsman, by breeding if not by birth. Catholic and Jacobite in a largely Protestant Scotland in the eighteenth century, the Fraser family suffered for its convictions. A kinsman, Lord Lovat, was beheaded on Tower Hill in 1747 for taking part in Jacobite uprisings; though Simon's grandfather, William, stayed clear of the fighting, his mansion was burned. Of William's nine sons, two fought with Wolfe at Quebec, and one stayed and made his fortune in Canada.

A large number of Roman Catholics left Scotland for America in 1773; among them was another of William's sons, Simon, who went first to New York, then settled in Vermont. When the colonies declared their independence in 1776, Simon signed on with the Loyalist forces. Like Mackenzie's father, he paid with his life: he was captured, badly treated, and died in prison not long after.

His eighth and youngest child, also named Simon, was born in Vermont in 1776. The death of the father left the family in trouble: their kin had joined the rebels and would not help a dead Loyalist's family. The Frasers suffered through conflicting claims to their land, through persecution and into poverty. In 1784, they moved north to Montreal. The sons who were old enough took up their own lands in Lower Canada; the widow, young Simon and several other brothers moved to land granted to them as Loyalists along the St. Lawrence in Cornwall Township, in the newly organized territory of Upper Canada.

Little is known of Fraser's life over the next ten years. When he was fourteen, he went to Montreal, where, it is thought, his uncle arranged a basic education for him and found him a job as a clerk in the North West Company offices; certainly he became an apprentice in the company in 1792. From there, he moved to the northwest; once or twice, he shows up in records as a clerk in the Athabasca department. But he must have done well. In 1801, at Grand Portage, just twenty-five years old, he was made a partner in the company, with a one-forty-sixth share.

If Fraser kept a journal of the next four years, it has not survived. But he must have followed the usual routine of wintering partners: travelling and trading through the northwest, spending the winters at one of the company posts, then coming to Grand Portage for meetings with the Montreal partners every June.

In the autumn of 1805, Fraser, with his clerks John Stuart and James McDougall and some twenty men, canoed up the Peace to the foot of the Peace River Canyon, where they built a post they named Rocky Mountain Portage House. Canoes would bring supplies up from Athabasca, for posts further west; voyageurs would bring furs obtained from the west to Rocky Mountain

Portage House, to be prepared and baled for transport to the east.

Fraser left Stuart in charge of building this post, and continued upstream with McDougall and a man named La Malice. Like Mackenzie, he turned south with the Parsnip River. He founded a second post, at McLeod Lake, naming it Fort McLeod. Three Nor'Westers were detailed to man the post over the winter; it was the first permanent non-native settlement west of the Rockies on the mainland of what is now British Columbia.

Fraser went back downriver to winter at Dunvegan, a long-established trading post. McDougall spent the winter exploring Carrier territory, travelling overland as far as Stuart Lake. Stuart remained at McLeod Lake. Early in 1806, Fraser returned to Rocky Mountain Portage House, prepared to extend the chain of trading posts farther west. Now thirty years old, he was a robust man with a heavy face and reddish hair, a man with more determination than education. His years in the north country had taught him how to face danger and hardship, and how to live off the land. He anticipated few problems in his new task.

Through April of 1806, Fraser waited for the ice to break up on the Peace, sending his men to the upper end of the portage with the packs of provisions and trade goods they would carry on their upcoming journey. Break-up came late. Only in mid-May did the packs of fur come downstream from Fort McLeod. Fraser quickly checked and repacked them, sent them off downriver to Dunvegan and closed off his own affairs at Rocky Mountain Portage House. At last, on May 20, he set off over the portage to the upper stretches of the Peace.

Fraser faced problems different from those that had confronted Mackenzie. A three-month dash and return through unknown territory, for all its dangers and difficulties, was one matter; establishing posts and holding the loyalty of clerks and traders who must stay in the wilderness over cold winters and mosquito-ridden summers was quite another. La Malice — "and never was a man better named" — caused Fraser endless problems. La Malice was living with a native woman, and insisted she come along on any exploring trip. Furthermore, he told Fraser, his contract with the North West Company did not oblige him to go any farther into the wilderness. Come with me, or go back to Montreal, Fraser insisted. In either case, do so without your woman. In the end, La Malice decided to tag along, *"par plaisir* but not *par obligation."*

From the beginning of his journey, Fraser seems to have had it in for Mackenzie, whom he snidely called "The Knight." Perhaps he had spent winters in the west hearing about the man who had feuded with his partners and gone over to the opposition; perhaps he had met Mackenzie and disliked him. And perhaps he was jealous of Mackenzie's reputation, or scornful of the edited memoirs that repeatedly showed Mackenzie in a heroic light. Whatever the reason, he rarely hesitated to criticize the man who had pioneered the route he now followed. "He seems to have been ambitious," Fraser wrote of Mackenzie as he canoed up the Finlay, "of having traced the Peace River to its source as well as confluence. This is not the only mistake

"I assure you I am tired of living on fish and I feel quite dull and lonesome since you left me. Nothing goes on to my likeing. I hate the place and the Indians. I will expect to hear from you again before you go to Trout Lake." — Fraser writes to John Stuart, September, 1808.

he seems to have committed, whether designedly or not I cannot say.... [Another comment by Mackenzie] makes me inclined to believe he has exaggerated all along, but then,'' in a sudden change of heart, "he was the first that passed, and it was pardonable in him, and I have not the least desire to detract from his merits.''

One of British Columbia's earliest historians, H.H. Bancroft, attributes Fraser's comments to his character. Bancroft terms Fraser "illiterate, ill-bred, bickering, fault-finding ... jealous, ambitious'' and blinded by prejudice. Whatever the reason, Fraser's comments enliven his journal, otherwise an unembroidered account of his travels.

Fraser and his men canoed up the Parsnip, then turned up the Pack River, as they had the year before. Mackenzie had

Foxes and other fur-bearing animals were abundant west of the Rockies; late in the eighteenth century, fur traders from the east began to advance on these new territories, seeking to replenish a dwindling eastern fur supply.

missed the Pack; he must, suggested Fraser uncharitably, have been napping when his canoe reached this point. "If I were inclined to find fault with him, I could prove he seldom or ever paid the attention he pretends to have done, and that many of his remarks were not made by him but communicated by his men,'' Fraser grumbled.

On June 7, eighteen days after they left the head of the Peace canyon, the men arrived at Fort McLeod, where they immediately set about making new canoes to replace the makeshift ones they had used to this point. It was not an easy job. Though they could split sufficient wood to make the ribs and frame, finding enough good birchbark to cover the frame was a long and difficult task. The weather turned cold, so the canoes could not be gummed until it warmed again. Stuart was the only practiced canoe-builder; the work progressed slowly. At last, after two weeks at Fort McLeod, the canoes were finished and Fraser embarked once more with his men.

La Malice now began to exact his revenge. He was hurt, he said; he was ill. He was, Fraser suspected, malingering. La Malice would not go on; he would not go back alone. "By all appearances,'' Fraser told his journal, "if he is really as bad as he pretends he will not live long.'' Of the twelve men in three canoes, six began to complain of sickness or assorted pains. La Malice accused Fraser and Stuart of holding a grudge against him. Fraser had had enough of the man, who had used up half the supply of medicine, and managed to eat a good portion of the food despite his many complaints. But what to do? Leave him behind alone? Not the action of kind

men. Leave another man with him? Unfair to the other man. In the end, they took La Malice along with them, and everyone was unhappy.

A week after they left Fort McLeod, retracing Mackenzie's route towards the Fraser, they met La Rancheuse, a Carrier who drew them maps of the surrounding country and said he knew a safer and shorter route westward. But Fraser chose instead to continue along Mackenzie's route, to the Bad River, which was just as bad as it had been thirteen years earlier. Cold

"The high hills, the precipices, the . . . ravines &c. rendered walking very painful and disagreeable. A pair of shoes does not last a day, and the men have their feet full of thorns." — June 6, 1808

Ridges and gullies caused hardship for members of the party travelling on foot. The terrain was so rugged that footwear needed constant repair.

The Fraser River above Quesnel is swift, but wide, with few obstacles. Here Fraser's party made good progress, and his journal comments on the abundance of game seen from the canoe. Although game is less plentiful now, deer still frequent the banks of the river.

and soaking wet, they battled the current, driftwood, roots, branches, stones, and rapids; one canoe was badly damaged in the river. Goods wet, men unhappy and exhausted, canoes now so heavy with gum that they could not be carried more than a few hundred metres at a time, provisions spoiling, they arrived at the Great River on July 10, seventeen days after they had left Fort McLeod.

Seabound explorers had identified the mouth of the Columbia; both Mackenzie and Fraser were convinced that the Great River was the Columbia. Exploring to the mouth of the river could wait; establishing a network of trading posts in this country was the first priority. They drifted for a day down the river to a fork, where the Nechako River entered. They worked their way up the Nechako against a current so strong that they had to pull themselves up, hand over hand, using the branches that hung out over the river. The days took on a routine: grinding upriver as one man bailed out water that leaked in through the spreading canoe seams, landing every few hours to repair and gum the canoes, spreading out the baggage and provisions to dry, returning to the river and starting the process over again, until rapids or other obstructions made it necessary to come ashore, empty the canoes, and portage farther up the river.

They reached the Stuart River and ascended it to Stuart Lake. The trip from Fort McLeod had taken more than a month; the route that La Rancheuse had talked about — and that Stuart had followed overland the year before — would have taken three and a half days. But Fraser was looking for a fur brigade route, and that meant a river route. Although the roundabout route was not suitable, he nonetheless set about building the post that would be named Fort St. James, under less than ideal conditions. He was short of provisions and trade goods; in any case, the Carriers at Stuart Lake had little food to trade. The salmon run was late in the spring of 1806,

"*As we were advancing inside of an Island, we saw two cubs in a tree and immediately pulled ashore to fire upon them, but before we could get to them they were off and La Garde and Barbuellen, who were the first on shore, pursued them. The latter soon met the mother and fired upon her to no effect, and she pursued him, in her turn . . . and as La Garde was advancing another bear suddenly rushed upon him and tore him in a shocking manner. Had not the dogs passed there at that moment, he would have been torn to pieces.*" — *July 13, 1808*

Early summer mornings on the Fraser can impart an eerie feeling to the silent forests, like this one near Soda Creek. It must have added to the sense of vulnerability and apprehension felt by the explorers in these unknown lands.

and the country around provided little other food.

Fraser supervised the building of the fort and did what little trading for furs he could. In August, he sent a letter off to the "gentlemen proprietors of the North West Company," reassuring them that the trade in this area would become profitable, since the natives were numerous and the country not destitute of beaver. But, he warned them, to succeed, he must soon receive more goods and better men.

Throughout that long summer of 1806 and the winter that followed, Fraser received neither the supplies nor the men he had requested. He sent Stuart off to explore the country south of Stuart Lake, then wrote to his clerk at Rocky Mountain Portage House that he was "tired of living on fish and quite dull and lonesome." He went down to join Stuart at Fraser Lake, where the men built another trading post and named it Fort Fraser. Fraser named the region New Caledonia; though he had never visited Scotland, the hills and forests reminded him of his mother's description of her homeland.

In December, Fraser returned to Fort St. James. With the beginnings of annoyance at the company, he wrote again, with heavy sarcasm, "it cannot displease you to hear of our being still safe, notwithstanding our not receiving any news or assistance from your quarter." He had planned, he said, to continue down the great river he thought was the Columbia, but "it would have been little short of madness . . . in a starving state without an ounce of any kind of provisions."

He had no decent canoes, no good men, no fresh provisions. Half the men who

> " *Here we are, in a strange Country, surrounded with dangers and difficulties . . . Our situation is critical and highly unpleasant; however we shall endeavour to make the best of it; what cannot be cured, must be endured." — June 15, 1808*

accompanied him were sick half the time. La Malice had never pleased him; now it seemed that McDougall had gone astray with native women and with the ethics of trading, so much so that Fraser wrote to him, "your character as a Trader [is] much blasted." Yet Fraser remained relatively cheerful. Despite his words to La Malice and McDougall, he wrote to Stuart that he had "once more entered upon the matrimonial state and you would have a hearty laugh if you heard of our courtship." By February, he had made plans for the summer of 1807. A supply of goods was to be brought over the three-day route to Stuart Lake; Fraser would then prepare for a trip down the Fraser. He wanted to send his journal back to company headquarters, but he knew it would not make a good impression. "It is," he wrote to Stuart, "exceedingly ill wrote worse worded & not well spelt." Perhaps, he asked, Stuart could do some editing; he may have had in mind the kind of alchemy he thought had been performed on Mackenzie's diaries, to bring him fame and some degree of fortune.

Two canoes carrying men and supplies finally arrived in New Caledonia from Dunvegan in the autumn of 1807. Though

In 1808, herds of Rocky Mountain elk, called Red Deer by Fraser, frequented the river below the confluence of the Fraser and Nechako rivers.

"*This country, which is interspersed with meadows and hills, dales and high rocks, has upon the whole a romantic but pleasant appearance.*" — *May 30, 1808*

it was now far too late in the year for Fraser to begin his long-planned-for trip to the coast, he could and did travel down to the junction of the Nechako and the Fraser, where he built Fort George. Though no record survives of the winter of 1807-8, not even mention of whether Fraser spent it at Fort George or Fort St. James, it undoubtedly followed the pattern of previous winters: short northern days, long freezing nights, boredom and the routine of trading for food and furs.

In the spring, their fur trading finished for another season, Fraser must have waited impatiently, day after day, for the ice to break up on the rivers, so that he could begin the journey he had been planning for three years. On May 28, Simon Fraser, his new clerk Jules Quesnel, John Stuart, nineteen voyageurs and two Indian hunter-guides set out down the Great River in two canoes. They ran through "romantic but pleasant" country, meeting en route natives who were little surprised by their arrival, who welcomed them, and who described for them the course of the river ahead. Within a day, they had entered new territory: Fraser had now passed the point where Mackenzie had turned back to seek a shorter route overland to the sea.

Fraser had been told that the natives along the way were peace-loving and friendly, but that those at the mouth of the river would be hostile and warlike. The natives he now met tried to convince Fraser that the river ahead was so rough, so rapid, and so constricted in places that an overland journey would be much preferable. But Fraser was stubborn. He was not convinced that the natives were telling him the truth — and he wanted very much to find a passable river route to the sea. His instructions were to follow such a river to the sea, to find out if it provided a possible trade route, and follow it he would.

Southwest of present-day Williams Lake, the men unloaded the canoes, and sent them, paddled by the best canoeists, through dangerous rapids. More by luck than by skill, the men came through alive and the canoes relatively undamaged. To pass the more treacherous rapids that now faced them, they cut steps in the steep

Fraser disregarded advice from local natives to leave the river and travel overland, around the rapids of the Fraser Canyon downstream. This placid section of the river near Williams Lake gives little hint of the fury to come.

By the time he had been on the river for three days, Fraser had passed from the cool forests of the Nechako to the arid lands of the Cariboo region. Here the forest is more open, and thick growths of grasses, like this foxtail barley, are interspersed with spring wildflowers.

ties apparently insurmountable, and they blamed us for venturing so far with our canoes & for not going by land as advised by the Old Chief on a former occasion, asserting this communication both by land & by water will in some places be found impracticable to strangers, as we shall have to ascend and descend mountains and precipices by means of rope ladders." But, since they had disregarded native advice to go overland, they must now proceed as well as they could by river.

The river did not improve. "This afternoon," Fraser recorded on June 9, "the rapids were very bad; two in particular were worse, if possible, than any we had hitherto met with, being a continual series of cascades, mixt with rocky fragments and bound by precipices and mountains, that seemed at time to have no end. I scarcely ever saw anything so dreary, and seldom so dangerous in any country; and at present while I am writing this, whatever way I turn, mountains upon mountains, whose summits are covered with eternal snows, close the gloomy scene."

The next day, after he sent two men downstream to examine the river's course, Fraser acknowledged the inevitable. The men built a scaffold for the canoes, and cached the provisions they would need when they returned. From now on, they must proceed on foot, or borrow canoes from whatever natives they met, to take them down the passable sections of the river.

At 5 A.M. on June 11, each man took up his thirty-five-kilo pack of "indispensable necessaries," and the group set off across ravines and along mountainsides, keeping as close to the river as the difficult

river banks and dragged and carried the canoes and goods past the rough water.

Rapids downstream now tested both men and canoes. One man lost his footing on a portage, and trapped himself and his pack between rocks. Fraser crawled out to extricate the man, but the pack shattered below them on the rocks of the river. Rapid succeeded rapid, precipice climbed on precipice. Fraser and his men emerged barely alive from one rapid where the cliffs on either side of the river made it impossible to portage. They were not encouraged by the local Atnah natives, who described the course of the river ahead: "[They] represented it as a dreadful chain of difficul-

terrain permitted. The Askettih Indians they now met were friendly, but they declined to lend Fraser and his men any of the horses they owned, and the group had to continue on foot, carrying their packs. Though the country was "the most savage that can be imagined," they had a beaten path to follow; though they were tired and disgruntled, they were not lost. They feared attack, but were almost overcome with native friendliness: at one village, near present-day Lillooet, Fraser had to shake hands with at least one hundred and thirty-seven men. He took advantage of the occasion to "impress upon their minds the numberless advantages which all nations in that quarter would derive from open communication with the white people." Until such advantages arrived, he asked for and got fish, roots and berries with which to feed his men.

He also obtained a canoe, for the Lillooet told him the river was navigable for a distance below their village. Several of the men took the heaviest goods downriver by canoe, while the rest walked overland, now hearing more and more often stories about the white men who had come in large canoes to the mouth of this river. They reached a fork in the river and Fraser named the blue waters that entered the muddy river the Thompson, for David

The Fraser party camped a short distance north of Lytton, then one of the largest native villages in the interior. Snow still clung to the peaks and the intense heat waves of the summer were a month away.

"*The Indians here are a mixture of Askittiks [Lillooet] and Hacamaugh [Thompson] Indians. They gave us a siffleur [marmot] which is the first fresh meat we tasted since our departure.*" — *June 17, 1808*

The Fraser River, seen here from Lillooet, is not easy to canoe. Rapids, whirlpools and vertical rock walls tested the fortitude and skill of the adventurers, but were still a mere hint of what lay ahead.

Thompson, his fellow Nor'Wester. They obtained another canoe, and everyone travelled by water, portaging only when no alternative existed.

Even when Fraser commanded them to portage, some of the men demurred. He and Stuart were in their tent one afternoon, writing, when they heard a sudden commotion. Rushing to the riverbank, they discovered the canoes had disappeared. They ran downriver, until, six kilometres farther on, they found D'Alaire, one of the voyageurs, soaked and exhausted. The men had decided that the portage they were attempting was too long, and had set the canoes into the river. D'Alaire's canoe filled with water and overturned, trapping the man underneath, struggling and spitting water. He managed to climb atop the canoe and ride the rapids as best he could. "In the second or third cascade," he reported, "the canoe from a great height plunged into the deep eddy at the foot, and striking with violence against the bottom, splitted in two. Here I lost my recollection." Regaining consciousness, D'Alaire rode what remained of the canoe through smoother water until a wave washed him ashore, and he was able to crawl up the steep, rocky bank to safer ground.

The Shuswap who saw the accident retrieved the other men and the remaining canoes. They now seemed to have decided that the white men were too foolish to learn the lesson of the river. "Knowing our indiscretion yesterday," Fraser wrote on June 22, "and dreading a like attempt, [they] voluntarily transported our canoes over land to a little river beyond the rapids." The local chief and The Little Fellow, a native who had travelled much

We had to pass where no human being should venture. Yet in those places there is a regular footpath impressed, or rather indented, by frequent travelling on the very rocks. And besides this, steps which are formed like a ladder, or the shrouds of a ship, by poles hanging to one another and crossed at certain distance with twigs and withes, suspended from the top to the foot of precipices, and fastened at both ends to stones and trees, furnished a safe and convenient passage to the Natives — but we, who had not the advantages of their experience, were often in imminent danger, when obliged to follow their example." — June 26, 1808

of the way with Fraser, promised they would stay with the expedition until it had passed all the rapids.

Fraser's men had finally run out of foolhardy courage: from daring impossible rapids, they now refused to try any at all, preferring to walk along the river's bank. Fraser tried to set an example by running several rapids, but the men were not convinced. Not that walking was without incident: one of the men fell and the canoe he was carrying shattered. They edged along the Fraser Canyon, paying heed to every instruction given by their guides. On one portage, the Thompson Indian guide climbed to the summit of an almost vertical hill and pulled the group up, one by one, with a long pole. Sometimes, noted Fraser,

Pictographs in the Stein Valley bear witness to a native presence predating the appearance of Europeans by hundreds of years. Fraser and his men were afforded a friendly greeting near here, shaking the hands of over a hundred people.

the path was so narrow "as to render it difficult for even one person to pass sideways."

He was, in fact, now thoroughly disillusioned with this river. Though the natives had worn a footpath along the almost-sheer sides of the Fraser Canyon, it was, said Fraser, a route no human should attempt. Yet attempt it they did, climbing and descending precarious pole-and-twig ladders, all the while marvelling at the skill of the natives, who made the trip without a single tremor.

Fraser needed canoes again, and the natives promised to get him some. But the canoes were at the head of the rapids, the men at the foot. The canoes could be neither portaged nor steered through the rapids, so the natives let them go at the top of the rapids and fished them out, miraculously still serviceable, though damaged, at the bottom. The men still marched by land, but the goods were transported by water.

The Fraser Canyon marked the end of the interior, the beginning of the coast, and the natives he now met were part of the Coast Salish nation. The river, too, had changed: it flowed through a broad valley. Hitchhiking in Salish canoes or borrowing the canoes from their owners, the group moved downstream, stopping at Salish villages en route, where they were usually treated to a meal and exchanged gifts.

On July 2, Fraser arrived at the destination he had so long sought. "At last," he wrote, "we came in sight of a gulph or bay of the sea; this the Indians called Pas-hil-roe. It runs in a S.W. & N.E. direction." Fraser had reached the mouth of the Fraser in the Strait of Georgia.

"The Natives without loss of time began to cross over in wooden canoes, and I had to shake hands with at least one hundred & thirty-seven men, while the old Chief was haranguing them about our good qualities ..." — June 14, 1808

The Salish farther up the valley had warned Fraser that they were at war with the coastal Musqueam. Beware, they said; don't stop. Fraser ignored the warnings, as usual, but soon found his valley friends were right. The Musqueam were less than friendly, less than welcoming, to this strange party that came downriver in the canoes of their enemies. They advanced to attack. Fraser and his men pushed them off with the muzzles of their guns, then paddled as quickly as they could upstream to the friendlier Salish village.

Fraser still wanted to see the main ocean, but the Salish no longer wanted to help. "We saw nothing but dangers and difficulties in our way," wrote Fraser, revealing once again how helpless he was without the assistance of the locals. "We, therefore, relinquished our design and directed our thoughts towards home."

The Salish refused to give him a canoe, so he took one by force, leaving its owner a blanket in trade or rent. One of Fraser's men, terrified by the confrontation with the natives, had run away. The party lost time looking for the runaway; the Salish chief, now unfriendly, soon caught up with them. Fraser managed to keep the peace with a display of angry words and gestures. But fear and disappointment were now his companions. "I must again acknowledge my great disappointment in not seeing the *main ocean*, having gone so near it as to be almost within view. For we wished very much to settle the situation with an observation for the longitude." He had established one fact: this river was not the Columbia. At forty-nine degrees latitude, the river mouth was much too far north to be the Columbia. If he had realized this sooner, Fraser wrote, he would have turned back at the head of the rapids where he had left his canoes three and a half weeks earlier.

Fraser might have spent more time musing had his situation been less desperate. The Salish villagers would neither lend them canoes nor trade them provisions. Some of the Salish tried to steal the group's possessions, perhaps having observed Fraser take a canoe without permission. Finally, Fraser managed to bargain for a canoe and set out again upriver, followed by several canoes of Salish who, if not warlike, were certainly not friendly. After a night's uneasy sleep on shore, several of the voyageurs decided they would not continue on the river, but would strike out overland, through unknown mountains, to return to the river north of the canyon.

Fraser remonstrated and threatened, but the men were adamant: they would rather risk possible death in the wilderness than court certain death on the river. Finally, Fraser prevailed. "After much debate on both sides, our delinquents yielded and we all shook hands, resolving never to separate during the voyage; which resolution was immediately confirmed by the following oath taken on the spot by each of the party: 'I solemnly swear before Almighty God that I shall sooner perish than forsake in distress any of our crew during the present voyage.' After this ceremony was over all hands dressed in their best apparel, and each took charge of his own bundle." They paddled off, singing at the tops of their voices.

Whether the oath would have been kept had further trouble threatened, we shall never know. The Salish fell back and the paddlers moved on, upriver into friendlier territory. By the next day, they had reached the foot of the Fraser canyon, where they were "received . . . with great kindness" by their old friends.

The return along the cliffs and the canyon terrified Fraser and his men as much as the downward journey. Again, they squeezed past rocks and through defiles, climbed precipices on native stick and branch ladders which swayed in the slightest breeze. Fraser recorded his gratitude: "The Indians deserve our thanks for their able assistance through these alarming situations. . . . [They] went up and down these wild places with the same agility as sailors do on board a ship."

On they went, back up the river, finding, on July 10, the untouched cache of provisions and the canoes they had left behind on their descent. On August 6, at noon, ten weeks after they had set out, Fraser and his companions returned to Fort George, at the confluence of the Fraser and Nechako rivers.

The rest of the trip was anticlimactic. They had undergone great hardship to prove a negative: the Great River was not the Columbia, and it could not be used as

a fur-trade route. Neither on the river nor overland along its banks could furs, provisions, and trade goods be easily carried. Fellow explorer David Thompson named this river the Fraser, in honour of the man who followed it to the sea, but the North West Company accorded Fraser little recognition.

In 1809, Fraser took a furlough away from the northwest, probably among family in Montreal or Cornwall. He returned to the northwest, but the records give us little clue about where he spent the next four years. He was assigned to the Athabasca district and once more became absorbed in the normal routine of the fur trade.

In 1814, he took another furlough. By this time, he was fed up with life in the wilderness, frustrated by the lack of recognition he had received, annoyed because his journals had not been published. He wanted to walk away from the company. But the North West Company was once more in turmoil, and many of the wintering partners wanted to be bought out. Montreal management told Fraser no money was

Travelling on foot as he approached the village at Lytton, Fraser was ferried across the Stein River by local natives. Today, the Fraser River ferry near here transports contemporary travellers. They are usually headed for the Stein Valley, drawn by wilderness and native pictographs to a place that many feel is a spiritual centre.

Below Yale the river is navigable again, as it flows into a wider valley. Fraser could once again travel by canoe, a relief from the dangers of the Fraser Canyon.

available to pay departing partners. Reluctantly, and with increasing bitterness, Fraser returned to the northwest. William McGillivray, a director of the company, wrote in 1815, "Mr. S. Fraser demurred about going to Athabasca, but after some altercation ... in which he was told he must go in or take the consequences, he finally acquiesced."

The company was now waging an undeclared war with the Hudson's Bay Company, and with Lord Selkirk, who had founded a colony at Red River. The Nor'Westers wanted the colony shut down; settlers could only interfere with the fur trade. Fraser was with Alexander Mackenzie, nephew of the explorer, when Mackenzie "persuaded" the colony's

ca at the time of the battle and was, he wrote, "not acquainted with the circumstances . . . of Governor Semple & several of his people having been destroyed by Half Breeds; upon my way out from Athabasca in the Spring to the Red River in the latter end of June last, Indians informed me of the fact." Fraser claimed he knew nothing of any violence planned by the North West Company against the settlers or the Hudson's Bay Company; he was aware, he said, that HBC men had burned and pillaged NWC property.

Selkirk was adamant. The North West partners arrested might not have been at Red River, but they must answer for the deaths they had encouraged by their hostility to the colony. Fraser and the other partners were sent to Canada for trial. En route, one of the canoes capsized, and nine of the twenty-one men drowned. In Montreal, the remaining men under arrest were released on bail. When they finally came to trial two years later, charged with treason and conspiracy, and as accessories to murder, all were acquitted.

Fraser never returned to the northwest. He settled in Stormont County, near Cornwall, where he married at the age of forty-four, and fathered five sons and three daughters. For twenty years, he farmed his land without great incident. In 1838, during the Upper Canada rebellion, a Loyalist in the tradition of his father, he served with the government forces and was injured in a fall. Unable to run his mill or his farm, he sought pensions from the colonial and the British governments, claiming his injury had reduced him to penury. He received only a colonial pension.

governor to depart; they took the governor to Fort William. Fraser then returned to Athabasca. In June of 1816, the new governor and sixteen settlers were killed in a battle with the Métis.

Lord Selkirk arrived at Fort William and arrested any North West Company partner he could find, among them Simon Fraser. Fraser protested: he had been in Athabas-

The Coast Mountains recede into the distance. Between Hope and the sea the Fraser River widens as it gathers in the tributaries that drain these snow-capped summits. For Fraser, travel on the river was now easier, but he was not to fulfil one goal — to see the open ocean past the river's mouth.

Fraser never received the recognition he thought due him for his explorations. Even now, no full-length biography has been written about him. In 1859, he and John McDonald, another survivor of the North West Company, drew up a declaration that, for the lack of any other, could well serve as Fraser's epitaph:

We are the last of the old N.W. Partners. We have known each other for many years. Which of the two survives the other we know not. We are both aged, we have lived in mutual esteem and fellowship, we have done our duty in the stations allotted us without fear, or reproach. We have braved many dangers, we have run many risks. We cannot accuse one another of any thing mean & dirty through life, nor done any disagreeable actions, nor wrong to others. We have been feared, loved & respected by natives. We have kept our men under subordination. We have thus lived long lives. We have both crossed this continent, we have explored many new points, we have met many new Tribes, we have run our Race, & as this is probably the last time we meet on earth, we part as we have lived in sincere friendship and mutual good will.

John McDonald died the year after the two men penned these words. Simon Fraser survived his old friend for two years. He died on August 18, 1862, at the age of eighty-six. His wife died one day later.

David Thompson: Completing the Land Map

Calypso orchids (Calypso bulbosa), *which appear soon after the snow melts each spring, can be found along the Blaeberry River, a major route used by Thompson to the headwaters of the Columbia.*

Alexander Mackenzie and Simon Fraser were intensely practical men, natural leaders who pursued their goals with few doubts. In the twenty years that they spent exploring the northwest, a different manner of man was making his own way across the uncharted muskeg, mountains and forests between Hudson Bay and the Pacific Ocean. David Thompson was to the map of northwest America what Cook had been to the charts of the Pacific. But Thompson's life was filled with far more contradictions and uncertainties than that of any of the other four explorers.

Thompson was born in London, to poor Welsh parents, in 1770. Two years later, his father died. When David was seven, his mother enrolled him in the Grey Coat charity school, whose "principall designe" was "to educate poor children in the principles of piety and virtue, and thereby lay a foundation for a sober and Christian life." The

Thompson negotiated some of the most difficult terrain of any of the major explorers in British Columbia. The towering summits and narrow passes of the central Rocky Mountains were his territory.

"In the month of May 1784 at the Port of London, I embarked in the ship Prince Rupert belonging to the Hudson's Bay Company, as apprentice and clerk to the said company ... Hudson's Straits were so full of ice, as to require the time of near a month to pass them...." — The preamble to David Thompson's Narrative.

school taught its boys mathematics, geography, reading, writing, and some of the basics of navigation, in preparation for life in the navy. But by the time Thompson was fourteen and ready to leave school, the navy had no need for apprentices. The school paid the Hudson's Bay Company five pounds to take the young man on as an apprentice.

Thompson arrived at Fort Prince of Wales on Hudson Bay in 1784. He was not impressed by the comfortless stone fort, built to replace two forts captured and burned by the French the year before. Winter came hard on the heels of the ship's arrival: for six months, wrote Thompson many years later, "all our movements were for self-preservation." There was wood enough for just one small fire in the morning, one in the evening. If the weather was bad the men walked the guard room, muffled in heavy beaver coats. Ten centimetres of frost clung to the walls; rocks split from the cold. Spring passed in a flash, marked only by the melting of the ice; summer brought "myriads of tormenting mosquitoes.... The narrow windows were so crowded with them," wrote Thompson, "they trod each other to death in such numbers, we had to sweep them out twice a day." With a budding scientist's curiosity, Thompson watched the insects through a microscope as they bit him, and described the process in detail.

Inquisitive and eager to learn, the young apprentice was given no difficult tasks; he was limited instead to growling at the cold, shooting birds and quarrelling with mosquitoes. Thompson, deeply religious, was equally unhappy with the fort's commander, Samuel Hearne, who declared a

volume of Voltaire his Bible and cohabited with a succession of native women. He was happy to be sent, in 1785, 230 kilometres south to York Fort, where he worked as a clerk, and wrote in his diary about the routine, the weather, the birds and animals of the region, all in carefully observed detail.

The following spring, he went inland to the new posts built by the company along the Saskatchewan River. He spent the winter of 1787-88 with the Piegan Indians, on the banks of the Bow River; almost every evening for four months, he sat and listened to Sarkamappee, a man of eighty or ninety, who described in detail the country in which he lived and Piegan habits, customs, manners, history, politics and religion. Thompson had found his first great teacher: by the end of the winter, he had a much greater understanding of both the land and its inhabitants, and spoke two Indian languages well.

Now eighteen years old, Thompson spent the next winter at Manchester House, on the North Saskatchewan River. He fell down a bank and broke his leg badly; the leg did not heal well, and he was forced to convalesce at Cumberland House, downstream. Bad luck turned to good in October, when trader and surveyor Philip Turnor arrived to survey the country west to the end of Athabasca Lake. "This was a fortunate arrival for me," Thompson wrote, "as Mr. Turnor was well versed in mathematics, was one of the compilers of the nautical Almanacs, and a practical astronomer." The knowledge Alexander Mackenzie travelled to London to acquire, Thompson learned in an isolated trading post. So fervently did he study, mostly by the light of one small candle, that he temporarily lost the sight of his right eye.

Sarkamappee and Turnor set Thompson on a track that would last the rest of his life. He yearned now to be away, surveying, enquiring, mapping. Over the next seven years, he crisscrossed what the traders called the Muskrat Country: that stretch of land and water southwest of York Factory, between the Churchill and the Saskatchewan. He paddled its rivers, rode on horseback across the land, walked thousands of kilometres through forest and across plains. Wherever he went, he recorded what he saw, making astronomical observations that enabled him to determine the latitude and longitude of his position with remarkable precision.

Yet, by the winter of 1796-7, Thompson was once more unhappy. Each year, the Hudson's Bay Company fur brigade travelled between York Factory and Cumberland House by way of a long, U-shaped route that took them far south, then north again by water. The company wanted to find a more direct path; Thompson, convinced he had discovered such a route, led seventeen men into the wilds in the fall of 1797. The trip was a dismal failure. The streams that Thompson was sure would carry them swiftly westward had dried to trickles that would scarcely admit a canoe loaded with only three light blankets; they would not serve for the heavily laden brigade canoes. Trapped by the terrain and the weather, the men were forced to winter at a cramped, makeshift post they built on the shores of a dismal lake. Half starving for want of provisions and lack of game they could shoot, they probably let Thompson know how they felt about his mistake.

Thompson had signed on for two further three-year terms with the HBC; on the second occasion, the governors had quadrupled his salary and spoken highly of him. He was slated to take over as Master to the Northward in the spring. The new job would mean he must pay more attention to the fur trade and less to exploration. But Thompson did not want to be den mother to other men in the fur trade; he wanted to be off on his own, exploring and mapping. During that winter at the wilderness lake, a trader from the rival North West Company stopped by. No one knows what he and Thompson discussed, but in April of 1797, he resigned from the company, and set out overland to join the Nor'Westers.

Thompson's superior, Malcolm Ross, was laconic about the departure of his assistant. "This morning," wrote Ross to the HBC governors, "Mr. David Thompson acquainted Me with his time being out with your Honours and thought himself a freeborn subject and at liberty to choose any service he thought to be most to his advantage and is to quit your service and enter the Canadian Company's employ."

Thompson was scarcely more loquacious. "I determined," he wrote years later, "to seek ... employment from the Company [of] Merchants of Canada, carrying on the fur trade under the name of the North West Company. With two natives, I proceeded to their nearest trading house ... and by the usual route of the canoes arrived at the Great Carrying Place on the north shore of Lake Superior."

Historians have accused Thompson of lack of loyalty to the company that had treated him well, and of opportunism.

"*I sat and listened to the old man [Sarkamappee] without being in the least tired, [his stories] were blended with the habits customs and manners, politics and religion ... anecdotes of Indian chiefs and the means of their gaining influence in war and peace that I always found something to interest me.*" — Winter, 1787-88.

Thompson travelled the wilderness in every season; snowy mountain scenes, like this in today's Jasper National Park, both oppressed him with the difficulties they presented and intrigued him with their beauty.

Though Thompson wrote little explaining his move, he had no doubts he was doing the right thing. He had tasted the spice of surveying and scientific observation; he wanted the full meal.

Whatever his ethics or motives, he did not regret his move. For the next year, he happily charted the country west from Grand Portage and the Great Lakes, across present-day Manitoba and Saskatchewan, into Alberta. He surveyed the forty-ninth parallel, to determine whether company posts lay in territory now declared to be in the United States, or in British territory. In early December of 1797, he travelled south towards the Missouri River, by dogsled across the "boundless plain." Severe cold and high winds plagued him and his companions; they were lucky to progress twenty kilometres a day. "We have taken thirty-three days to perform a journey of ten days in good weather," he wrote. But, he added, ever the surveyor, "[this] has given me the opportunity of determining the latitude of six different places, and the longitude of three."

After a long visit with the Mandan Indians, whom he described in detail, he returned north, calculated his results and drew a map which he forwarded to company headquarters. He then snowshoed south again, switching to canoe travel as soon as the ice broke up. On April 27, 1798, having crossed the height of land between the rivers that flowed to the north and those that ran to the south, he decided a lake he found was the source of the Mississippi River. He was wrong — but only by a few kilometres.

The North West Company, like the HBC, was most interested in making money from

Rocky Mountain goats are famous for their sure-footedness on steep, rocky terrain. Thompson's one shipment of goat skins met with scorn from his eastern partners. When they later expressed interest, Thompson refused to supply more skins: the animals were too difficult to hunt, and he had been piqued by the earlier rebuffs.

mind: unlike almost any other explorer, Thompson took his family with him on many of his travels.

The Nor'Westers now sent Thompson farther west, into the shadow of the Rocky Mountains. Despite their earlier refusal to take Mackenzie's proposals seriously, the company did want to find trade routes across the Rockies. In 1800 and 1801, Thompson and Duncan McGillivray probed from the prairies into the foothills to the mountains beyond, seeking a pass that would allow them easy passage to the west. "To the westward," Thompson wrote on one occasion, "hills and rocks rose to our view covered with snow, here rising, there subsiding, but their tops nearly of an equal height everywhere. Never before did I behold so just, so perfect a resemblance to the waves of the ocean in wintry storm."

McGillivray, exhausted and ill, was forced to return east. Thompson was instructed to cross the mountains and follow the Columbia River to the sea. He doubted that he could. "The arrangements were such that I saw plainly that the whole thing was hopeless." He thought the only available guide was fearful, uncertain and dishonest. But he would try, nonetheless; he set out with the guide and helpers, carrying enough birchbark with them to make a canoe once they arrived on the far side of the Rockies.

They followed the Saskatchewan River upstream on horseback, over wet and broken ground and woods burned and tumbled, then through the swift-moving river. Rain hammered down on them; "the water descended in sheets from the hills, and flooded the country; the river at all times rapid was now an overflowing

furs. Now they directed Thompson, as had the HBC before them, to spend his time increasing the profits of the company. Over the next five years, Thompson continued his travels east of the Rockies, but he did so as a trader, bringing the fur brigade canoes down to the annual rendezvous and returning to various posts to trade for furs.

In 1799, he met and married Charlotte Small, the fourteen-year-old daughter of a wintering partner and his Indian wife. Unlike other fur traders, Thompson, a Christian who took his religion seriously, solemnized his marriage in a church ceremony; it would be for life, not for the length of his stay in the west. He rarely refers to his wife or, as they arrived, his children, but they were never far from his

"*About one third of a mile from us lay an enormous Glacier, the eastern face of which quite steep, of about two thousand feet in height, was of a clean fine green color, which I much admired.''*
— *January 10, 1811*

Glaciers along their route unnerved Thompson's men as they crossed the Rockies in midwinter via Athabasca Pass, a prime place and time for avalanches.

Autumn scene, Rocky Mountain Trench. Thompson was greatly interested in the natural surroundings of the territories he explored. His journals contain numerous references to flora and fauna and reveal an appreciation for wilderness areas unusual for explorers of the time.

torrent that bore down on everything that opposed its course. The thunder rolled along the hills and added horror to the darkness of the night. We wished for the morning light.''

The next morning, they followed a brook deep into the mountains, where metre-deep snow still covered the ground. The brook led them to a lake wedged between two mountainsides; the horses could go no further. Thompson and one of his men crawled and slithered along the lakeshore and beyond, cutting their shoes to pieces on the sharp rocks. At last, they reached a brook that, they decided, would lead them back to the Saskatchewan River. They returned to the rest of the party, planning to send the horses back with the guide. The men were to take up light packs and go back to the river by this new-found path via lake and brook.

The men saw it differently; they did not want to risk their lives. Though Thompson wanted the men to be braver, he conceded that ''it was improbable that they could have got down the mountain with the baggage without at least one-half of them being crippled.'' Unlike Mackenzie, Thompson was all too ready to see his men's point of view, all too uncertain of his own. They turned back the way they had come, to the Saskatchewan, where they built canoes for a new attempt on the mountains. But it was no more successful than the old. ''The river was everywhere bounded by crags, whose height was never less than 300 feet, and often rose to 500 feet perpendicular above the level of the river. Here then, for the present, was my last hope destroyed.'' The men turned the canoes around, and the current swept them the 120 kilometres to Rocky Mountain House in less than six hours.

The failure distressed Thompson. But, he said, he had learned his lesson: he needed better men and fewer, he must get a guide from the western side of the mountains, and he must not take horses.

Thompson's chance to use what he had learned did not come for six more years. The battle between the North West Company and its rivals drained energy and resources away from any venture into new territory. From 1801 to 1806, Thompson worked and traded in his old territory, the Muskrat Country along the Athabasca. When the North West Company merged with its enemies, it was Simon Fraser who was instructed to find a way west, from the Peace River, not the Saskatchewan.

In 1806, Thompson left the Muskrat Country for the last time, going overland to Fort William. There he was instructed to try once more to open trade relations with the Indians across the Rockies in the southern part of British territory. That year, he wintered at Rocky Mountain House. He sent trader Jaco Finlay into the mountains to build a trail west that horses could follow. In the spring, as the ice left the rivers, he ventured once more up the North Saskatchewan. One group went by canoe; Thompson, his family, and three others rode on horseback.

Thompson left the horses at Kootenay Plain, a broad expanse of grass where the Kutenai often camped, and continued upriver, into the mountains. "Here, among these stupendous solitary wilds covered with eternal snow," he recorded, "and mountain connected to mountain by immense glaciers, the collections of ages,

Wilderness travellers know that a deep turquoise colour warns of icy water: the colour is caused by finely ground particles of "rock flour" suspended in glacial waters. The murky waters conceal deep spots and cause debilitating leg cramps, dangers that were almost a daily occurrence for Thompson in his mountain journeys.

Thompson searched the valleys around the Saskatchewan River for a route through the Rockies, finally settling on Howse Pass. He made the journey in June, when snow is still deep in the passes, and lakes such as Waterfowl Lake, above, are just becoming ice-free.

on which the beams of the sun make hardly any impression.... I stayed for fourteen days more, impatiently waiting the melting of the snows on the height of land.... Wearied with waiting and anxious to proceed, contrary to the opinion of everyone, I set off.... By 10 a.m., we were at the head of the defile where the springs send their rills to the Pacific. This sight overjoyed me." Thompson had confirmed a way through the Rockies.

He sent back for his family, his men and his horses. The group crossed the Great Divide by way of what is now known as Howse Pass, and followed a brook that swelled from a gentle rivulet to a raging torrent in the five days that it took them to descend to the valley from the pass. Just north of present-day Golden, he reached the Columbia River.

Just as Fraser had mistaken the Fraser for the Columbia, so Thompson was unable to recognize the Columbia for itself — a failure understandable to anyone who looks at the roundabout path the Columbia takes from source to sea. Thompson was not pleased with his situation. Almost out of food and weary from their travels, they arrived at Windermere Lake not far from despair. "I found myself necessitated to lay aside all thoughts of discovery for the present and bend my whole aim to an establishment for trade ... and as our pressing necessities did not allow time for thought upon thought, I set out to look for a place where we might build, that ... I might be at liberty to seize every favourable opportunity of extending my knowledge of the country."

When a band of Kutenai arrived, they saw the travellers' "famished looks and

asked no questions," but donated food to the hungry group and traded them dried and fresh meat. The Kutenai warned Thompson that the site he had chosen was too far from fresh water and too vulnerable to attack; Thompson moved south to Toby Creek, where he and his men built Kootenae House: "Log Houses . . . strongly stockaded . . . on three sides, the other side resting on the steep bank of the River. . . . The stockades were all ball proof, as well as the Logs of the Houses."

For Thompson expected trouble. His old friends, the Piegan, were not at all happy that he and his fellow traders were now supplying the Kutenai, traditional enemies of the Piegan, with goods and weapons.

"The water, from the melting of the snow in the Mountains, had risen upwards of six feet; and overflowed all the extensive fine meadows of this country." — May 14, 1808

Yearly spring overflows of the Kootenay River resulted in the rich soils and wildlife habitat of the Creston Valley.

The Piegan had threatened — and Thompson expected them to try to make good their threat — to kill Thompson and his men.

Though deer and antelope were plentiful, the men had little success shooting either. They resorted to eating several of their horses and some wild horses, descended from Spanish horses traded to the Indians farther south, but disliked the oily taste. At length, salmon appeared in the river, on the last leg of their nineteen-hundred-kilometre journey from the sea. "As the place where they spawned had . . . swift clear water on it," wrote Thompson, "we often looked at them, the female with her head cleared away the gravel, and made a hole to deposit her spawn in, of perhaps an inch or more in depth, by a foot in length, which done, the male then passed over it several times, when both covered the hole well up with gravel." The salmon were good fresh, or smoked over a fire of aspen or wood from other deciduous trees, but harsh and unpleasant when smoked over pine wood. For three weeks, they lived on fish, but once the salmon spawned, "they became poor and uneatable," and the men returned to horse meat.

Two canoes of trade goods arrived, too late for any more to be done that year. As soon as the mountains were passable in the spring, Thompson sent off the furs he had collected over the winter, among them

Whitetail deer, elk and moose were found along the Kootenay River, but Thompson and his men had little success in hunting. They were forced to rely on salmon, supplies they had packed in and wild horse meat to survive.

"one hundred of the Mountain Goat skins with their long silky hair, of a foot in length of a white colour, tinged at the lower end with a very light shade of yellow." He was ridiculed for doing so by "some of the ignorant self sufficient partners." When the skins sold well, at a good price in London, the partners asked for more, but it was not in Thompson's nature to forgive: "for their ignorant ridicule I would send no more, and I kept my word," he wrote.

When a Piegan party visited the fort, Thompson was sure they wanted to destroy the buildings and the people in them, to preserve their position as middlemen in the trade between white and other tribes. Thompson spoke persuasively and gave the Piegan gifts. "In all that regarded the Piegan," he congratulated himself, "I chanced to be right. . . . Intimately acquainted with the Indians, the country and the seasons, I argued and acted on probabilities." But at heart, he was convinced only Providence stood between them and the ire of the Piegan.

He therefore decided to move out of range. He left the Columbia, crossing the brief, low ridge of land to what we now know as the Kootenay River. Where banks constricted the stream, Thompson "found it full of small whirlpools of about two inches in diameter, all in motion, drifting with the current." He could find no cause for the phenomenon.

Following the river downstream, the group encountered rough water: "violent eddies and whirlpools . . . threatened us with sure destruction . . . which we escaped by hard paddling, keeping in the middle of the River." Late in April they killed "an animal of the tiger species" —

a cougar, one would think. Thompson described the beast in detail, and repeated the Indian reports of its habits. The meat was good, he said, though the two who ate the liver suffered from a violent headache for several hours afterwards.

They reached present-day Montana, but their travel was soon curtailed by rising waters fed by mountain snow melt that overflowed into the bottom lands along the river. He engaged two natives with one canoe, to take them back across the flooded land, then bought horses when they could no longer proceed by water. Their guide decamped; the floods had made the usual routes impassable, and Thompson did not know how he could return to Kootenae House. As ever, he put his trust in God, praying "to the Almighty to relieve" them.

Provided by faith or coincidence, a Kutenai chief took pity on them and agreed to act as their guide. When they reached

According to native legend, these towering hoodoo formations, below, are the ribs of a gigantic fish that tried to make its way north through Columbia Lake and died at the north end, near present-day Dutch Creek. Thompson passed this way many times in his travels to and from the Kootenay River south of the lake.

the Moyie River, running fast and overflowing its banks, the guide told them they must make a canoe and venture out on the river. "Hungry and tired, with heavy hearts, we set to work, and got the materials ready to put together the next morning." Then the guide reconnoitered and reconsidered: he led them overland, across "rude rocks and patches of pathless woods." A Kutenai family they met fed them with dried trout, a kilogram of dried meat and four cakes of bread made from the fine black moss that grew on fir and larch trunks.

Climbing and descending, wading through water up to their waists, cutting trees to build bridges across fast-flowing rivers, they made slow progress towards their goal. The Moyie almost defeated them: every tree they threw across it was swept away by the current. They worked their way upriver to a place where the river was divided into five channels. Four could be crossed, but the fifth was more difficult. Thompson had a hundred and thirty-five kilograms of fine furs that would be damaged by water; they tied everything into small parcels and gingerly hauled them across on a line made from buffalo hide. But buffalo hide weakens in water, and a large parcel of beaver hides and some of the men's baggage was swept away when the line broke. Nonetheless, they were safe and Thompson thanked kind Providence that they were quit of "this terrible River."

Thompson had learned his lesson: travelling in spring when the rivers flooded the flatlands was next to impossible.

Back at Kootenae House, they baled up the furs acquired in the winter's trading, and started back across the Rockies. Thompson left wife and family at Rocky Mountain House, and continued east to Rainy River House, the depot for furs collected in the far west. He turned west again, picked up his family, and recrossed the Rockies. For the next two years, he devoted himself to trading, perhaps spurred by a desire to assure his growing family of a good living. "It is my wish," he wrote to a friend in 1810, "to give all my children [he was to have a total of thirteen] an equal and good education; my conscience obliges it and it is for this I am now working in this country."

Whatever his dedication to trade, he would not transgress his principles. On his return from Rainy River, he was forced to take two kegs of alcohol with him, to trade for furs. "I had made it a Law unto myself, that no alcohol should pass the Mountains in my company, and thus be clear of the sad sight of drunkenness, and it's many evils," he wrote. "When we came to the defiles of the Mountains, I placed the two Kegs of Alcohol on a vicious Horse; by noon the Kegs were empty, and in pieces, the Horse rubbing his load against the Rocks to get rid of it." But Thompson

"I left the Kootenae House on the 20th of April, proceeded to the Lakes, the scources of the Columbia River, carried everything about two miles across a fine plain [Canal Flats] to McGillivray's River, on which we embarked." — April 20, 1808

Canal Flats is a flat, marshy area that separates the source of the Columbia, Columbia Lake, from the Kootenay River. For years, Thompson thought that the Kootenay was the Columbia. The real Columbia — which Thompson named Kootenay — was just a few kilometres away.

The Moyie River runs swift and cold in the springtime. Thompson made the crossing then and lost some pelts and supplies to the raging waters.

did not deceive his partners about his acts of righteousness. "I wrote to my partners what I had done; and that I would do the same to every Keg of Alcohol, and for the next six years I had charge of the fur trade on the west side of the Mountains, no further attempt was made to introduce spiritous Liquors."

Thompson wintered at Kootenae House, passing his time by trading, hunting ducks, taking observations of such things as a brilliant mock sun that shone on December 22, and making notes on birds and other wildlife. In March, he decided to attempt a task he had long wanted to try:

ascertaining the height of the mountains around him. Twice a mountain barometer sent to him with the brigade canoes had been broken on the journey; now he would use his own calculations. By a careful process of observation and deduction, he estimated that nearby Mount Nelson was 3936 metres above sea level; it is in fact 3637 metres high. His main mistake: over-estimating the amount the Columbia — whose route he still did not know — fell between its source and the sea.

Though his calculations might be slightly askew, his observations were acute. "On the steep, bare sides of these mountains," he wrote many years later, "I twice saw the first formation of the clouds of a storm. Its first direction was from the Pacific Ocean, eastward up the valley of the lower Columbia River, and McGillivray's River, from which the Hills forced it from east to north; the Sun was shining on these steep Rocks when the clouds of the Storm entered about 2000 feet above the level ground; in large revolving circles, the northern edge of the circle behind cutting in it's revolution the centre of the circle before it, and this circle within circle for nearly twenty miles along these high Hills until the clouds closed on me and all was obscurity; it was a grand sight."

The following spring, he followed the brigade route again, returning to Kootenae House in mid-August. From there, he travelled to present-day Idaho and Montana, building Kulyspell House and Saleesh House, where he spent the winter. Twice he tried to find a route west; though he could not know it, he was less than fifty kilometres from the Columbia.

Early in May, Thompson set out for Kootenae House with his brigade of canoes. Their return to the Saskatchewan was relatively uneventful, though a wolverine had chewed through the pine logs and bark that protected their cache, and eaten eleven kilograms of pemmican, half a dressed leather skin, and three pairs of shoes.

He continued on to Rainy River House, taking his wife and children with him. Since he was already two years overdue for a scheduled year's leave, he probably planned to continue on to Canada. What awaited him at Rainy River House? We cannot be sure. Some historians say his superiors told him to return to the west

"We soon came to a deep River with a strong current overflowing the low grounds. . . . Early next morning we commenced cutting large Cedars and Pines to fall across the River . . . but the torrent was so rapid, that every tree we threw across the stream was either broken by the Torrent or swept away. . . . We crossed swimming our Horses and thus thank kind Providence, crossed and got clear of this terrible River by sun set." — May 26-27, 1808

and follow the Columbia to its mouth, fore-stalling American traders who had pledged to build posts at the river's mouth. Others say no such instructions were ever issued: Thompson was to return west, and continue working his way slowly along the river, establishing posts and good relations with the natives as he went. But Thompson himself recorded that the arrival of the American traders on the Columbia changed everything: "I was now obliged to take 4 canoes and to proceed to the mouth of the Columbia to oppose them."

Whatever his instructions, he returned west and started out to cross the mountains. What happened next no one living knows, though the evidence suggests that Thompson either left or was somehow separated from his men, and took refuge from a Piegan party that was determined to keep him and his men from crossing the Rockies. Alexander Henry, a fellow trader, reported that he found Thompson near a

"The same Brooks which cost us so much hard work and were crossed with danger [in spring], in Autumn have very little water; and almost everywhere fordable, the water not a foot in depth." — June 3, 1808

tributary of the Saskatchewan River, on the top of a hill, above the water, his tent well hidden in the trees. He had been there almost four weeks. Afraid to fire his gun lest the Piegan find him, he was out of food and almost starving.

Did Thompson, terrified, desert his men and wait to be rescued by men braver than he? Did he take the only prudent course, keeping out of the way of his enemies until they departed? We do not know. We do know that Thompson now sought a different route across the Rockies, north of Piegan territory. Twenty-four horses and twenty-four men worked their way north, heavy-laden with provisions, tents and trade goods, through the cypress forests, windfalls and meadows east of the mountains. On the twenty-ninth of November, after a month's travel, they reached the Athabasca River. Four days later, with winter approaching, they sent back most of their horses and continued on foot with their dogs.

For another month, they hunted, and made snowshoes and dogsleds. On December 30, they set out over snow and ice, up the Athabasca towards the mountains. They left their remaining horses at the last

meadow where the horses could feed. On January 10, 1811, they came to the height of land between the Atlantic and Pacific oceans. "It was to me a most exhilarating sight," wrote Thompson, "but to an uneducated man, a dreadful sight.... My men were the most hardy that could be picked out of a hundred brave hardy men, but the scene of desolation before us was dreadful, and I knew it." The men grew despondent and frightened, "yet when night came they admired the brilliancy of the stars, and as one of them said, he thought he could almost touch them with his hand." And Thompson himself could not help dwelling more on the natural than the human world: he described the glacier that lay not far from their camp, and the snow deep within a hole the men bored: "the color of the sides of a beautiful blue; the surface was of a very light color, but as it descended the color became more deep, and at the lowest point was of a blue, almost black.

"Many reflections came on my mind," he continued. "A new world was in a manner before me and my object was to be at the Pacific Ocean before the month of August. How were we to find Provisions, and how many Men would remain with me, for they were dispirited? Amidst various thoughts, I fell asleep on my bed of Snow." Thompson was endowed with far less bravado and far more introspection than any of his fellow land explorers.

They descended the west side of the mountains, slipping and sliding through wet, heavy snow, to the banks of the Columbia, where he thought to build a canoe and follow the river's windings to the sea. They camped near the junction of the Wood, the Canoe and the Columbia, today's Boat Encampment. He was overawed by the trees around them; on the east side of the mountains, he wrote "we were men, but on the west side we were pigmies." Those same trees, more than forty metres high and almost thirteen metres around, and the snow around them that never thawed, disheartened his companions, "eight hardy Canadians." Four deserted; "I was not sorry to be rid of them," concluded Thompson, "as for more than a month past they had been very useless, in short they became an incumbrance on me." There was no cajoling, no threatening: Thompson would not deny his companions the right to leave, if they so wished.

The men remaining lined a hole in the deep snow with cedar boards and roofed it over: this would be their temporary home. They managed to shoot a few deer, and dried the meat for their upcoming journey; the deer skins they deemed to be useless, since they had "no woman to dress them." They were delighted to find many fine birch trees, and looked forward to making a canoe. But the birch rind was too thin, and they were forced instead to

Fall brings lower water levels to the rivers, making crossings easier. Game is also plentiful, and Thompson made many hunting forays throughout the southern Rocky Mountain Trench.

Looking west from Saskatchewan Crossing, Icefields Parkway, Jasper National Park. Thick bush and a long uphill climb characterize the route to the Athabasca Pass, which Thompson crossed in the dead of winter. This is not a hospitable place at the best of times, but he chose it to avoid contact with the Piegan, who Thompson thought were trying to prevent his crossing of the mountains.

" *The east side of the Mountains is formed of long slopes, very few in this defile that are steep; but the west side is more abrupt, and has many places that require steady sure footed Horses, to descend it's banks in the open season; one is tempted to enquire what may be the volume of water contained in the immense quantities of snow brought to, and lodged on, the Mountains, from the Pacific Ocean, and how from an Ocean of salt water the immense evaporation constantly going on is pure fresh water; these are mysterious operations on a scale so vast that the human mind is lost in the contemplation." — January 13, 1811*

construct a canoe of cedar boards sewn together with pine tree roots.

Thompson decided to go upriver instead of down, then carry across to the Kootenay River — which he still believed to be the main stream of the Columbia — and follow it down to the ocean. They left on April 17; almost a month later, they crossed the divide to the Kootenay and Kootenae House, four hundred and fifty kilometres from the winter hut. They continued down the Kootenay to a path that led to Clark's Fork River, in present-day Montana. From Clark's Fork, they canoed, then rode, then canoed again, from river to river, from trading post to trading post. On July 3, they reached the main stream of the Columbia.

The journey downriver was peaceful, broken by visits with native groups whose

villages lay along the river banks. On July 12, they saw and shot at seals that had followed spawning salmon upriver. The next day, they reached Point Vancouver, "from which place to the sea, the river has been surveyed by Lieut. Broughton, R.N., and well described by him." On July 14, they reached the mouth of the Columbia and looked out over the ocean, "To me [it] was a great pleasure," Thompson wrote, "but my men seemed disappointed. They had been accustomed to the boundless horizon of the great lakes of Canada, and their high rolling waves; from the ocean, they expected a more boundless view, a something beyond the power of their senses which they could not describe, and my informing them that directly opposite to us, at the distance of five thousand miles, was the empire of Japan, added nothing to their ideas, but," his faith in chart-making strong, "a map would."

They paddled another few kilometres to the trading post established at the Columbia mouth by John Jacob Astor, the aggressive American fur merchant who had arrived just four months earlier. They stayed with Astor for a week, then started back up the river. If the intention of the North West Company had been to forestall the Americans, they were just too late.

Thompson and his men paddled back up the Columbia, branched off on the Spokane River, then returned to the Columbia at Kettle Falls. Thompson's diary for this part of the trip is missing; his surviving notebooks indicate the men worked their way up the Columbia to the Arrow Lakes, paddled north through the lakes, then followed the Columbia back to the winter hut at the mouth of the Canoe River. They

"*As usual, when the fire was made I set off to examine the country before us, and found we had now to descend the west side of the Mountains; I returned and found part of my Men with a Pole of twenty feet in length boring the snow to find the bottom: I told them while we had good Snow Shoes it was no matter to us whether the snow was ten or one hundred feet deep.*" — *January 10, 1811*

Thompson travelled up the Athabasca River and eventually into Athabasca Pass by dog team. This was the easy part of the journey, before the terrain steepened and the route became confined to a narrow valley bordered with hanging glaciers.

expected to find men from across the mountains waiting for them with supplies, but no one was there. They paddled up the Canoe, hoping to meet their friends, but returned to the Columbia alone and empty-handed. Then two men brought news from across the mountains, and Thompson rediscovered his resolve. He went east, battling through "snow so deep at the height of land that with difficulty the horses got through it; and in one place they had to pass the night up to their bellies in snow, and the next morning were so discouraged that it was some time before we could get them to a steady walk." Yet they were back on the west side of the Rockies by October 13, with trade goods and provisions for the upcoming winter.

Thompson spent the winter of 1811 exploring south through Montana. In spring, he went back up the Columbia with a brigade of six canoes loaded with furs. On May 5, he arrived at Boat Encampment; he left the men to dry and pack the furs, and to cross the mountains as soon as they were ready and the weather permitted. Having made for themselves "bear paws, which are roughly made snow shoes round at each end," he set off with three hunters to cross the mountains. "On the eighth at noon," he wrote, "we gained the height of land, having with great labour ascended the hills which were under deep snow mixed with icicles from the dropping of the trees, which made very severe walking." He had sent men on ahead; on May 11, 1812, they returned with horses, and all continued to the nearest company post.

Thompson had crossed the Rockies for the last time. Now years overdue for his leave, he took his wife and family east to

Fort William, for the annual meeting of the wintering partners and Montreal agents. He was ready to retire. His partners appreciated what he had done. For his services, he was voted a full share of the profits for three years, plus a hundred pounds a year. The hundred pounds would pay him to "finish his charts, maps, &c. and deliver them to the agents in that time, after which he [was] to be considered as a retired partner and enjoy the profits of one hundredth for seven years."

In June, 1812, the United States declared war on Great Britain. The news set Fort

The Columbia overflows its banks in spring, resulting in a fringe of small ponds along most of its length. The ponds provided excellent habitat for waterfowl near Thompson's Kootenae House headquarters. Thompson, who had hunted for food and recreation while at posts for the Hudson's Bay Company, was an excellent marksman.

William alight with anxiety; men scurried to send off the winter's furs and to get themselves down to Montreal.

"We had only a short distance to dread being captured," between Sault Ste. Marie and Lake Huron, Thompson wrote. The danger safely passed, the voyageurs, Thompson, and his family crossed to the Ottawa River and to Montreal.

Settling near Montreal, Thompson carefully completed his map of the northwest territory, marking in their correct places lakes, rivers, mountains, portages, passes, and North West Company posts between Hudson Bay and the Pacific, from the Columbia to Lake Athabasca — territory he had charted in his twenty-eight years and eighty thousand kilometres of travel on foot, by horseback, and by canoe. Though Thompson received little credit at the time for his work, his map served as the basis for every map of the region he knew so intimately until the twentieth century.

In 1815, the war over, Thompson and his family moved to Upper Canada. For eleven years, he was British astronomer and surveyor on the commission set up to survey the border between Canada and the United States, from Montreal to Lake of the Woods. He then retired to life as a farmer.

Thompson might have been content to stay on his farm — but he could not afford to. Stories abound about the causes of his debts and ensuing poverty.

Some say he set his sons up in business, then assumed their debts when they failed. Others suggest he forgave debts owed to him, then was forced into bankruptcy himself. Whatever the cause, the result was evident. In 1833, sixty-three years old, Thompson was forced to return to surveying. He continued working, mapping areas along the St. Lawrence, in the eastern townships of Quebec, and in the Muskoka Lakes country, until he was almost seventy.

Then, still debt-ridden, he began to write a narrative of his travels, hoping the book would bring him enough money to escape from poverty. His hopes were not realized. Blind from glaucoma for the last nine years of his life, he could not finish editing the journals, and he and his wife had to live on donations from a son-in-law.

He died, poor and little recognized, in 1857, at the age of eighty-seven. His wife, Charlotte, lived on for just three more months. His journals, unfinished, were finally published in 1916. Only in this century did he begin to achieve some measure of recognition for the surveys that filled in much of the map of Northwest America.

The Purcells rise above the Kootenay River. They block the course of the Columbia River and cause it to make a long detour northward before turning south towards the Pacific Ocean. The river's route was the source of Thompson's confusion between the Kootenay and Columbia rivers.

BIBLIOGRAPHY

The Journals

Cook, James, et al. *The Voyage of the Resolution and Discovery, 1776-1780*. (J.C. Beaglehole, ed.) Cambridge: Cambridge University Press, for the Hakluyt Society, 1967.

Fraser, Simon. *Letters and Journals, 1806-1808*. (W. Kaye Lamb, ed.) Toronto: the Macmillan Company of Canada Limited, 1960.

Mackenzie, Alexander. *The Journals and Letters of Sir Alexander Mackenzie*. (W. Kaye Lamb, ed.) Cambridge: Cambridge University Press, for the Hakluyt Society, 1970.

Thompson, David. *David Thompson's Narrative, 1784-1812*. (Richard Glover, ed.) Toronto: The Champlain Society, 1962.

Vancouver, George. *The Voyage of George Vancouver, 1791-1795*. (W. Kaye Lamb, ed.) London: The Hakluyt Society, 1984.

Selected References

Anderson, Bern. *Surveyor of the Sea: the Life and Voyages of Captain George Vancouver*. Toronto: University of Toronto Press, 1960.

Bancroft, H.H. *History of British Columbia, 1792-1887*. New York: McGraw Hill, [c. 1967?].

Beaglehole, J.C. *Life of Captain James Cook*. Stanford, Calif.: Stanford University Press, 1974.

Fisher, Robin, and Johnston, Hugh (eds.). *Captain James Cook and His Times*. Vancouver: Douglas and McIntyre, 1979.

Hopwood, Victor G. (ed.). *David Thompson: Travels in Western North America, 1784-1812*. Toronto: Macmillan of Canada, 1971.

Morice, A.G. *History of the Northern Interior of British Columbia*. Toronto: William Briggs, 1904.

Rodger, N.A.M. *The Wooden World: an Anatomy of the Georgian Navy*. Glasgow: William Collins Sons & Co., 1986.

Walbran, Captain John T. *British Columbia Coast Names 1592-1908*. Vancouver: J.J. Douglas, for the Vancouver Public Library, 1971.

INDEX